Instructor's Manual to Accompany

Philosophy
THE POWER OF IDEAS

Fourth Edition

Dan Barnett
Brooke Noel Moore
Kenneth Bruder

California State University, Chico

Mayfield Publishing Company
Mountain View, California
London • Toronto

International Standard Book Number: 1-55934-989-1

Manufactured in the United States of America

10   9   8   7   6   5   4   3   2   1

Mayfield Publishing Company
1280 Villa Street
Mountain View, California 94041

Contents

SECTION I CLASS PRESENTATION MATERIALS

SECTION II OBJECTIVE QUESTIONS

Introduction

We do several things in this guide to make life a little easier for you. Specifically, for each chapter of the text we do this:

First, we provide a list of the main points of each chapter. With these lists you can review the chapters without having to reread the chapters in their entirety. You can also use the lists as outlines for lectures, if you want. You can even copy them and place them on the lectern in front of you.

Second, we list the various boxes that appear in each chapter, and provide a brief statement about their contents (except where the contents are obvious). In this text, many of the boxes contain important concepts and principles and distinctions, and not just amusing anecdotes. So you will want to know what's in them without having to thumb through the text.

Third, we list the reading selections for each chapter, with a brief description of the contents of each selection.

Fourth, if you are like us, you may want to have handy the names of the principal works of the philosophers you mention in lectures or discussion. So we made lists of the main works of the philosophers mentioned in each chapter; you can place these on your table or lectern while you are talking. Or you can use them for overheads.

Fifth, we offer some remarks that we hope may be useful to you in constructing lectures and stimulating class discussions. These remarks are related to one or two of the questions asked in the text at the end of each chapter (other than the first, which is introductory).

Finally, we supply a complete bank of objective test questions at the back of the manual. (These test items are available in a computerized format; please contact your Mayfield representative for details.) The questions are not a substitute for the philosophical essay, but they can be useful in gauging students' grasp of a reading assignment. One instructor uses short objective quizzes in a group setting to stimulate discussion among his students.

Overview of the Text

The text contains separate historical overviews of metaphysics and epistemology (including the Continental, pragmatic, and analytic traditions), ethics and political philosophy, and philosophy of religion (with an emphasis on proofs for the existence of God). The fourth part of the book turns topical in its consideration of post-modern critiques, including those from Continental, feminist, and post-colonial perspectives, with a chapter devoted to the development and influence of Eastern philosophy and religion (including Hinduism, Buddhism, and Confucianism).

Although the organization of this text was largely determined by the kind of beginning philosophy course we like to teach, the text can be adapted to suit different teaching strategies. Before we can say anything about that, however, you should have a clearer idea of what the text contains.

• Chapter 1, **Powerful Ideas.** This is an introductory chapter. In it we emphasize the power and importance of philosophy. Discussed are several representative philosophical questions—the problem of change, and the problem of whether we are ever really morally blameworthy for what we do. We also explain some of the various ways of subdividing philosophy: by branches, periods, subject, geography, and "traditions." In addition, we say something about the benefits of philosophy, dispel a couple of false ideas that beginning students are apt to have about the subject, and consider the nature of philosophical argumentation. A brief discussion of common mistakes in reasoning rounds out the chapter.

Part 1: Metaphysics and Epistemology: Existence and Knowledge

• Chapter 2, **Early Philosophy.** This chapter examines the views of the pre-Socratics, including Thales, Anaximenes, Anaximander, Pythagoras, Heraclitus, Parmenides, Zeno, Empedocles, Anaxagoras, and the Atomists.

• Chapter 3, **Socrates, Plato, and Aristotle.** The focus is on the central figures in the development of the Western philosophical tradition, with an emphasis on Plato's doctrine of the Forms and his theory of knowledge.

• Chapter 4, **The Philosophers of the Hellenistic and Christian Eras.** From metaphysics in the Roman Empire (including Plotinus, St. Augustine and Hypatia) we turn to the Middle Ages and the Christian philosophy of St. Thomas Aquinas.

• Chapter 5, **The Modern Period.** Here we explain several metaphysical and epistemological perspectives: that of Descartes and dualism, Hobbes and materialism, Anne Conway and Spinoza and their alternative monadologies, Locke and representative realism, and Berkeley and idealism.

• Chapter 6, **The Eighteenth and Nineteenth Centuries.** This chapter treats Hume and Kant in the eighteenth century, and Hegel in the nineteenth. We explain that Kant's epistemological skepticism was turned into metaphysical idealism by Hegel and the other Absolute Idealists, and look at the reactions of Schopenhauer, Kierkegaard, and Nietzsche. Finally, by contrast, we consider the empiricist premises of John Stuart Mill.

   • Chapter 7, **The Continental Tradition.** We focus in this chapter on the existentialism of Camus and Sartre and the phenomenology of Husserl and Heidegger. (Chapter 13 covers hermeneutics, deconstruction, and critical theory.)

   • Chapter 8, **The Pragmatic and Analytic Traditions.** Here we examine the pragmatism of Peirce, William James, and Dewey, and the development of philosophical analysis in the work of Russell, G. E. Moore, Wittgenstein, and Quine. We also provide a treatment of the philosophy of mind from the broadly analytic perspective.

Part 2: Moral and Political Philosophy

   • Chapter 9, **Moral Philosophy.** In this chapter we look first at the ethical thought of Plato and Aesara, the Lucanian, as well as that of Aristotle, the Epicureans, and the Stoics. Christian ethics is represented by the thought of St. Augustine, St. Hildegard of Bingen, Heloise and Abelard, and St. Thomas Aquinas. Finally we turn to Hobbes and Hume, and stress that ethics "after Hume" is the working out of options left open by Hume's moral philosophy. We conclude the chapter with a study of Kant, the utilitarians, and Nietzsche.

   • Chapter 10, **Political Philosophy.** This chapter concentrates on the political theory of Plato and Aristotle, the natural law theory of Augustine and Aquinas, the contractarian theories of Hobbes, Locke, and Rousseau. We present Mary Wollstonecraft's arguments against Rousseau's view of women, then proceed to American Constitutional theory, the classic liberalism of Harriet Taylor and John Stuart Mill, utopianism, and Marxism.

   • Chapter 11, **Recent Moral and Political Philosophy.** Here we present the contemporary ethical theories of G. E. Moore, W. D. Ross, and the emotivists, and discuss whether the "naturalist fallacy" is really a fallacy. We cover John Rawls's political liberalism, Robert Nozick's libertarianism, communitarian responses to Rawls and Alasdair MacIntyre's virtue ethics. We finish the chapter with a consideration of feminist moral theory, including the views of Susan Moller Okin on justice, gender, and the family, and the Marxist political philosophy of Herbert Marcuse.

Part 3: Philosophy of Religion: Reason and Faith

   • Chapter 12, **Philosophy and Belief in God.** Our concern in this chapter is the question of God's existence. We cover the basic arguments and classic objections, starting with Anselm and Aquinas, Descartes, Leibniz, Hume, and Kant. There is also a section on the mystical tradition of knowing God. We consider the nineteenth-century perspectives of Newman, Kierkegaard, Nietzsche, and William James, and conclude with two twentieth-century views: that of logical positivism, which argues that the question of God's existence is not a meaningful question; and that of Mary Daly, who calls for replacing the traditional patriarchal (and oppressive) image of God with a more liberating one.

Part 4: Post-Modern Critique

> • Chapter 13, **An Era of Suspicion.** This chapter presents the social critiques of Habermas and critical theory, Foucault's "archeological" and "genealogical" projects, structuralism and deconstruction, and Rorty's questioning of the use of such words as "Truth" and "objectivity." We close with an examination of how language can perpetuate sexism and how feminist epistemology and ecofeminism are developing new challenges to traditional philosophical perspectives.

> • Chapter 14, **Eastern Influences.** In this chapter we consider the development of Hinduism and Buddhism in India; Taoism, Confucianism, and Ch'an Buddhism in China; and Zen Buddhism and the Samurai tradition in Japan. We conclude with remarks on the influence of both Confucian and Zen Buddhist traditions.

> • Chapter 15, **Other Voices.** In this chapter we consider the historical background of post-colonial thought, focusing on African philosophy; native American, African-American, and Latin American thought; and the thought of South Asia (with an emphasis on Mohandas K. Gandhi and Rabindranath Tagore).

Appendixes

> • Appendix 1: **Truth.** Sets forth the principal philosophical theories of truth (including the correspondence and coherence theories) with a look also at the pragmatic and performative theories of truth.

> • Appendix 2: **Knowledge.** Discusses answers to the question "What is knowledge?" Plato's view is considered, as well as the claim in some recent epistemology that knowledge is "justified true belief."

Readings

The text also contains original readings. As mentioned in the preface, we think beginning students in philosophy ought to read original material, but we must be careful not to overwhelm them with difficult technical writing. The selections in this text are reasonably challenging, but not impossibly difficult. Your class will be the best judge of whether we have found the right compromise between formidability and triviality.

In case you need information now about the selections to determine how best to use this book, in the Class Presentation section of this instructor's guide we list and briefly summarize the selections, chapter by chapter.

Adapting the Book to Different Teaching Strategies

The book is used most comfortably with the teaching approach we favor, which is to acquaint our students with the histories of the various branches and subjects of philosophy. We like this approach because, as we explained in the preface to the text, it seems to us to make it easier for our students to follow themes.

Still, though, the text is adaptable to other teaching strategies. If you prefer to teach a history of philosophical figures, you might focus on Part 1, metaphysics and epistemology, since a very large number of the important philosophers are covered in it. Your students might then read the other parts of the book as supplementary material. Or, if you prefer not to give metaphysics and epistemology a predominant position in your course, you might focus on one of the other parts of the text, making it the "main" material.

If you use a problems approach in your class, the chances are that the problems you select will be from two or three of the branches of philosophy. This text will enable your students to acquire a background in the history of just those branches without having to read a history of the entire discipline of philosophy. Of course, if you want them to read a history of the entire discipline as background, this text should also give you what you need.

SECTION I

CLASS PRESENTATION MATERIALS

CHAPTER 1

Powerful Ideas

Main Points

1. The word *philosophy* comes from two Greek words, *philein* (which means "to love") and *sophia* (which means "knowledge" or "wisdom").

2. For ancient Greek thinkers, "philosophy" was a word that could describe the careful consideration of any subject matter (such as what today we would call physics or psychology). Today mathematics, the physical and biological sciences, economics and political science, theology, and many other areas have become disciplines of their own.

3. <u>Philosophical Questions</u>

   Philosophy today mines a rich vein of fundamental questions unanswered by other fields of knowledge, such as "What is truth?" "Is it possible to know anything with absolute certainty?" "Do people really have free will?" "What kind of person should I be?" "What is the proper role and function of the state?" and "Is there a God?"

4. Consideration of these fundamental questions grows out of everyday experience: use of a Styrofoam cup may raise the issue of one's moral obligation to the environment; a science-fiction movie about robots might suggest an exploration of the idea that such mechanisms have real feelings.

5. What makes a question a philosophical question is itself a philosophical issue. It is clear, however, that philosophy is not an empirical science.

6. Many questions that are philosophical are normative questions about the value of something. What are the norms of beauty? What are the norms of morality? How are they to be established?

7. Other philosophical questions concern the nature of change. If something changes, is it different from the way it was, and, if so, is it the same thing? The implications are more than just theoretical. If a woman on death row who is about to be executed announces she has had a change of heart, and now believes in God, is she a different person? Is that a good reason to stop the execution?

8. Some philosophical questions arise from commonsense beliefs that seem to conflict. If causes make effects happen, then are voluntary choices also caused? If they are, it would seem such choices had to have happened, but that conflicts with the idea of voluntary. If they are not, that runs counter to the idea that every event (including every voluntary choice) is caused. Should a person receive praise for acting in a way that could not have been otherwise? Should a person receive praise for doing something she did not cause?

9. The Divisions of Philosophy

   Seven branches of philosophy: metaphysics, epistemology, ethics or moral philosophy, social philosophy, political philosophy, aesthetics, and logic.

10. Historical subdivisions: ancient (sixth century B.C. through about the third century A.D.); medieval (fourth through sixteenth centuries); modern (fifteenth through nineteenth centuries); contemporary (twentieth century and beyond).

11. Philosophy-of-discipline areas: philosophy of science, philosophy of mathematics, philosophy of law, philosophy of education, and so on.

12. Philosophy-of-subject areas: philosophy of mind, philosophy of sports, philosophy of religion, feminist philosophy, philosophy of love, and so on.

13. Geographical divisions: Eastern and Western philosophy, with subdivisions such as American philosophy, Scandinavian philosophy, and the like.

14. Twentieth-century "traditions": Analytic philosophy (involving the practice of philosophical analysis) and Continental philosophy (including existentialism, phenomenology, hermeneutics, deconstruction, and critical theory).

15. The Benefits of Philosophy

   The benefits of philosophy: the search for answers to inherently interesting questions; development of logical and critical thinking skills and the ability to spot hidden assumptions; and less likelihood of being trapped by uncritical dogmatism.

16. Two Myths About Philosophy

    Two myths about philosophy: any opinion is as good as any other opinion (but philosophy requires reasoned support for its claims); philosophy is light reading (but generally the opposite is the case).

17. Arguments

    When someone supports a belief by giving a reason for accepting the belief, that person has given an argument. The conclusion of the argument is the point the person is trying to establish; the reason or reasons the person gives for accepting the conclusion is given by the premises of the argument.

18. The two ways an argument can fail: (1) one or more of the premises might be questionable and (2) even if the premises are not questionable, they might fail to support or establish the conclusion (logic is concerned with this second type of failure).

19. Common Fallacies (Mistakes in Reasoning)

    Argumentum ad hominem ("argument to the person"): the attempt to discredit a view by discrediting the person holding the view.

20. Appeals to emotion: arguments that try to establish conclusions solely by attempting to arouse or play on the emotions of a listener or reader.

21. Straw man: the alleged refutation of a view by the refutation of a misrepresentation of that view.

22. Red herring: a general term for those arguments that address a point other than the one that is at issue. Ad hominem, appeals to emotion, and straw man can all be seen as specific types of red herrings.

23. Begging the question: more or less assuming the very thing that the argument is intended to prove.

24. Black-or-white fallacy (false dilemma): an argument that assumes there are only two options when in fact other options exist.

Boxes

- Should You Want to Study Philosophy?
  (An ancient Pythagorean philosopher says "yes," for that is the way of wisdom)

- Philosophical Concerns in North America Today
  (Ethical issues in business, law, and medicine as professions; the question of whether machines can think; the nature of rationality; social implications of abortion, euthanasia, and informed consent; feminist issues; questions of social and economic justice; the nature of personhood; and other issues)

- Which Came First, the Chicken or the Egg?
  (If a tree falls in the forest and no one is around, does it make a sound?)

- Philosophy Never Makes Progress
  (A gentle response to those who charge that philosophical questions are unanswerable and that the discipline makes no progress)

- Comments on Philosophy
  (Some intriguing quotations)

- Philosophy and a Philosophy
  (The difference between philosophy as a discipline and one's personal philosophy)

- Side Benefits
  (Why those who have doctorates in philosophy are less likely to be unemployed than even chemists and biologists)

- Personal Truth
  (Beliefs may be personal, but truth is not)

CHAPTER 2

Early Philosophy

Main Points

1. **Epistemology** is the branch of philosophy concerned primarily with the nature, sources, limits, and criteria of knowledge. In the history of philosophy, epistemology and metaphysics have been intimately connected.

2. "**Metaphysics**," the term, in its original meaning refers to those untitled writings of Aristotle "after the *Physics*" that deal with subjects more abstract and difficult to understand than those examined in the *Physics*

3. The fundamental question of Aristotle's metaphysics, and therefore of metaphysics as a subject, is *What is the nature of being?* However, this question was asked before Aristotle, so he was not the first metaphysician. In addition, it has admitted a variety of interpretations over the centuries, though for most philosophers it does not include such subjects as astral projection, UFOs, or psychic surgery.

4. The first Western philosophers are known collectively as the **pre-Socratics**, a loose chronological term applying to those Greek philosophers who lived before Socrates (c. 470–399 B.C.).

5. The thinking of these early philosophers ushered in a perspective that made possible a deep understanding of the natural world. Advanced civilization is the direct consequence of the Greek discovery of mathematics and the Greek invention of philosophy.

6. The Milesians

    Thales conceived and looked for (and is said to be the first to do so) a basic stuff out of which all is constituted. He pronounced it to be water.

7. Thales also introduced a perspective that was not mythological in character. He saw the world naturalistically, consisting of substance and process.

8. **Anaximenes** pronounced it to be air.

9. **Anaximander** thought it must be more elementary than water or air, and to be ageless, boundless, and indeterminate.

10. Pythagoras

    Pythagoras is said to have maintained that things are numbers, but, more accurately (according to his wife Theano), Pythagoras meant that things are things because they can be enumerated. If something can be counted, it is a thing (whether physical or not).

11. For Pythagoras, there is an intimacy between things and numbers. Things participate in the universe of order and harmony. This led to the concept that fundamental reality is eternal, unchanging, and accessible only to reason.

12. Heraclitus and Parmenides

    Heraclitus looked for the essential feature of reality and said that all is fire, whose nature is ceaseless change determined by a cosmic order he called the *logos*, through which there is a harmonious union of opposites.

13. Parmenides deduced from a priori principles that being is a changeless, single, permanent, indivisible, and undifferentiated whole. Motion and generation are impossible, for if being itself were to change it would become something different. But what is different from being is non-being, and non-being just plain isn't.

14. Empedocles and Anaxagoras

    Empedocles, reconciling Heraclitus's and Parmenides's views, recognized change in objects but said they were composed of change*less* basic material particles: earth, air, fire, water. The apparent changes in the objects of experience were in reality changes in the positions of the basic particles. He also recognized basic forces of change, love and strife.

15. **Anaxagoras** introduced philosophy to Athens, and introduced into metaphysics the distinction between matter and mind. He held that the formation of the world resulted from rotary motion induced in mass by mind = reason = *nous*.

16. Mind did not create matter, but only acted on it, and did not act out of purpose or objective. Unlike Empedocles, Anaxagoras believed matter was composed of particles that were infinitely divisible.

17. The Atomists

    Leucippus and **Democritus**: All things are composed of minute, imperceptible, indestructible, indivisible, eternal, and uncreated particles, differing in size, shape, and perhaps weight. Atoms are infinite in number and eternally in motion.

18. The Atomists distinguished inherent and noninherent qualities of everyday objects: color and taste are not really "in" objects, though other qualities, such as weight and hardness, are.

19. The Atomists held that because things move, empty space must be real.

20. The Atomists were determinists. They believed that atoms operate in strict accordance with physical laws. They said future motions would be completely predictable for anyone with enough knowledge about the shapes, sizes, locations, directions, and velocities of the atoms.

21. The common thread of the pre-Socratics: all believed that the world we experience is merely a manifestation of a more fundamental, underlying reality.

Boxes

- Being?
  (Some of the various questions a philosopher might have in mind when he or she asks, What is the Nature of Being?)

- Olives
  (Thales shows a philosopher can be practical)

- Pythagoras and the Pythagoreans

- On Rabbits and Motion
  (Two of Zeno's antimotion arguments explained)

- Mythology
  (The legacy of ancient myths and their influence on philosophy, psychology, and literature)

- Democritus

- Free Will Versus Determinism
  (Common sense believes in both, but they seem to be in conflict)

Philosophers' Principal Works

- Thales (c. 640–546 B.C.)

- Anaximander (c. 611–547 B.C.)
  On the Nature of Things

- Anaximenes (c. 585–528 B.C.)

- Pythagoras (c. 582–507 B.C.)

- Theano of Croton (sixth century B.C.)
  On Piety

- Heraclitus (c. 535–475 B.C.)

- Parmenides (fifth century B.C.)

- Zeno (334–262 B.C.)

- Empedocles (c. 495–435 B.C.)
  On the Nature of Things
  Purifications

- Anaxagoras (c. 500–428 B.C.)

- Democritus (460–370 B.C.)
  Little World System
  On Nature
  In the Nature of Man

- Leucippus (mid-fifth century B.C.)
  On Mind

Lecture-Discussion Ideas Related to Selected Questions

6. A note on Parmenides and the Atomists.

For Parmenides, the only alternative to being was non-being (nonexistence), so that if being itself could undergo change of any kind (that is, could be different in some way from what it was originally), the only way for being to be different would be for it not to exist. But that is logically absurd, for being cannot be and not-be at the same time. Thus, it is impossible for being to change.

The Atomists used the idea of a "void" (the Greek word is *kenon*, the Latin word *vacuum*) to give "room" for things (atoms) to undergo change. But empty space was also real. A helpful way to understand this is to note that while the void was "nothing" (no-thing), it was not non-being. So for the Atomists both things and no-things existed: both had being (as opposed to non-being).

```
┌─────────────────────────────────────────────────────────────────┐
│                          Parmenides                               │
│   BEING                                        NON-BEING           │
│   IS                                           IS NOT              │
│                                                                   │
└─────────────────────────────────────────────────────────────────┘
```

```
┌─────────────────────────────────────────────────────────────────┐
│                         The Atomists                              │
│   BEING                                        NON-BEING           │
│   Thing (Body)                                 IS NOT             │
│   No-Thing (Void)                                                 │
│   IS                                                              │
└─────────────────────────────────────────────────────────────────┘
```

Source: Unknown

8.   *"The behavior of atoms is governed entirely by physical laws." "Humans have free will." Are these statements incompatible? Explain.*

We don't believe they ever invented a beginning philosophy student who doubted free will. So regardless of your own views on the subject, it can't hurt to argue against the idea. If it does nothing else, it will help students to see that the idea that we have free will is not the self-evident thing that it seems.

A good way to begin is by stipulating that Smith has free will if and only if it was physically possible for her to have acted differently in the same circumstances. Hence: if she has free will then it was physically possible for the atoms in the parts of her body that moved when she acted to have moved differently in the same circumstances. And if the atoms could have moved differently in the same circumstances, then they are not governed by physical laws. So, if they are governed, then she doesn't have free will.

Possibly someone will ask, and even if nobody does ask the subject should be brought up anyway, why it is that, if it was possible for something physical to have behaved differently in the same circumstances, then it was not governed by physical law. The answer is that that's what it is to be governed by physical law. Take a simple law, for example, water boils at 100 degrees Celsius. What it means to say that that is a law is that if you raise the temperature of some water to 100 degrees it will boil. If you could raise the water to 100 degrees without its boiling, then it wouldn't be a law that water boils at that temperature.

A rejoinder might be—and few students will raise it, though you might—that it is consistent with the idea that the activity of *subatomic entities* is governed by physical laws that there are "uncaused events" in the subatomic realm, and that therefore a subatomic entity could have behaved differently in exactly the same circumstances even though it is governed by physical laws. It might then further be suggested that if subatomic entities could have behaved differently in the same circumstances while being governed by physical laws then so could atoms and larger things, such as Smith's arms and legs, since subatomic entities exist in these atoms and larger things.

However, let's set aside the scientific controversies involved in this rejoinder, and suppose that the atoms in Smith's arms, while being governed by physical laws, could have moved differently due to the "uncaused" activity of internal subatomic entities. The point is, so what? True, it would follow that Smith has free will, as defined above, for she could have acted differently in the same circumstances (at least her body parts could have moved differently). But if she had acted differently, it would have been due to the "uncaused activity" of subatomic particles within her body, and not due to *her*.

This is a good place to bring forth the old dilemma: Either your act was caused, or it wasn't. If it was, then it couldn't have *not* happened. And if it wasn't, then *you* didn't cause it. Either way, you can't be held to account for your act.

CHAPTER 3

Socrates, Plato, and Aristotle

Main Points

1. Plato (c. 427–347 B.C.) was the pupil of Socrates (470–399 B.C.), and Aristotle (384–332 B.C.) was the pupil of Plato.

2. <u>Socrates</u>

    Socrates was not interested in arguing with his fellow Athenians merely for the sake of argument—as the Sophists were—but rather he wanted to discover the essential nature of knowledge, justice, beauty, goodness, and the virtues (such as courage).

3. The Socratic (**dialectic**) method: a search for the proper definition of a thing that will not permit refutation under Socratic questioning. The method does not imply that the questioner already knows the proper definition, only that the questioner is skilled at detecting misconceptions and at revealing them by asking the right questions.

4. Socrates was famous for his courage and for his staunch opposition to injustice. The story of his trial and subsequent death by drinking hemlock after his conviction for "corrupting" young men and not believing in the city's gods is told in Plato's dialogues *Apology, Crito,* and *Phaedo.*

5. <u>Plato</u>

    <u>Plato's metaphysics: the Theory of Forms.</u> What is truly real is not the objects of sensory experience but the **Forms** or **Ideas**. These are not just in the head but are in a separate realm and are ageless, eternal, unchanging, unmoving, and indivisible. Circularity and beauty are examples of Forms.

6. Particular objects have a lesser reality that can only approximate the ultimate reality of Forms. A thing is beautiful only to the extent it participates in the Form *beauty*, and is circular only if it participates in the Form *circularity*.

7. Plato introduced into Western thought a *two-realms* concept of a "sensible," changing world (a source of error, illusion, and ignorance) and a world of Forms that is unchanging (the source of all reality and all true knowledge). This Platonic dualism was incorporated into Christianity and today still affects our views on virtually every subject.

8. Some Forms, notably the Forms *truth, beauty,* and *goodness,* are of a higher order than other Forms. The Form *circularity* is beautiful, but the Form *beauty* is not circular.

9. <u>Plato's theory of knowledge.</u> Plato developed the first comprehensive theory of knowledge in philosophy, though many of his predecessors had implicit epistemological theories, some of them based in skepticism.

10. A **skeptic** is someone who doubts that knowledge is possible. **Xenophanes** declared that even if truth were stated it would not be known. **Heraclitus** believed that just as one cannot step into the same river twice, everything is in flux; though he himself did not deduce skeptical conclusions from his metaphysical theory, it does suggest that it is impossible to discover any fixed truth beyond what the theory itself expresses. **Cratylus** argued that a person cannot step even once into the same river because the person and the river are continually changing. True communication is impossible since words change their meaning even as they are spoken. It seems to follow that knowledge would also be impossible.

11. The Sophists, who could make a plausible case for any position, seemed to support skepticism by implicitly teaching that one idea is as valid as the next. **Gorgias** said there was no reality, and if there were, it could not be known or communicated; **Protagoras**, the best-known Sophist philosopher, maintained that "man is the measure of all things." Plato took this to mean that there is no absolute knowledge since one person's view of the world is as valid as any other's.

12. In his dialogue *Theaetetus*, Plato argued that if Protagoras were correct, the person who viewed Protagoras's theory as false would also be correct. Plato also argued against the popular notion that knowledge can be equated with sense perception. Knowledge clearly involves thinking and the use of concepts that cut across individual sense perceptions. Knowledge can be retained even after a person's particular sense experience ends. Besides, since the objects of sense perception are always changing, and knowledge is concerned with what is truly real, sense perception cannot be knowledge.

13. For Plato, the objects of true knowledge are the Forms, which are apprehended by reason. (Perfect beauty or absolute goodness cannot be perceived.)

14. Plato's epistemology is summarized in a passage in the *Republic* called the Theory of the Divided Line, which contrasts true knowledge with mere belief or opinion.

15. Aristotle

    Aristotle observed nature closely and came to be considered the definitive authority on all subjects except religion (on which, nevertheless, his impact came to be tremendous and long-lasting).

16. Aristotle called metaphysics "first philosophy." For him, to be is to be a particular thing, and each thing is composed of *matter* in a particular *form*; with the exception of God, neither form nor matter is ever found in isolation from the other. There is no separate and superior realm of Forms.

17. Aristotle: The basic questions that can be asked of any thing are about its causes, which are four: the formal cause (the form of the thing), the material cause (what it is made of), the efficient cause (what made it), and the final cause (its purpose or end).

18. Change can be viewed as movement from potentiality to actuality. Because actuality is the source of change, pure actuality (that is, the unchanged changer, or God) is the ultimate source of change.

19. Aristotle maintained that the metaphysics of his predecessors was concerned with various kinds of causation (Thales with material causation, Plato with formal causation, Empedocles and Anaxagoras with efficient causation). It was for Aristotle to provide an adequate explanation of final causation.

20. Aristotle used what is called the **Third Man argument** to take issue with Plato's Theory of Forms. Circular coins have the Form *circularity* in common; but an additional Form is needed, it seems, to express what one of the coins and the Form circularity have in common. And there needs to be yet another Form to express what the additional Form and the Form of circularity have in common, and so on.

21. Aristotle's own view is that the forms are universals (something that more than one individual can be) but that such universals do not exist apart from particulars. Circularity has no independent existence apart from particular circular things.

22. Aristotle's contribution to the study of sound reasoning is fundamentally important, and he is known as the father of logic. His work on the syllogism (where one proposition is inferred from two others) is still taught in universities throughout the world. (To *infer* one proposition from other propositions is to see that the first one *follows from* the others.)

23. Aristotle's logic is linked to his metaphysics because he believed that the forms of thought in which we think about reality represent the way reality actually is.

Boxes

- Profile: Aristocles, a.k.a. "Plato"

- The Cave
  (Plato's famous allegory designed to explain his two-realms philosophy)

- What Is Truth?
  (No, this box doesn't have the answer. It just refers the reader to Appendix 1. Sorry: the appendix doesn't have the answer either.)

- Profile: Aristotle

- Aristotle and the Deaf
  (Aristotle's harmful idea that the blind were more intelligent than the deaf)

Readings

3.1   Plato, from *Republic*

An account of the Good, the Divided Line, the Myth of the Cave, and the work of philosophers in the ideal society.

3.2   Plato, from *Meno*

Plato's view that knowledge about reality comes from within the soul through a form of "recollection," and that the soul is immortal.

Philosophers' Principal Works

- Socrates (c. 470–399 B.C.)

- Plato (c. 427–347 B.C.)
  Republic
  Theaetetus
  Symposium
  Parmenides
  Timaeus
  Apology
  Crito
  Phaedo

- Aristotle (384–322 B.C.)
  Physics
  Metaphysics
  *On the Soul (*De Anima*)*
  Nicomachean Ethics
  Politics
  The Organon of logical works

Lecture-Discussion Ideas Related to Selected Questions

4.   *Does a world of Forms exist separately from the world of concrete, individual things? Explain.*

We have had good luck with the following three techniques for selling Plato's Forms to our students. We don't claim originality for any of them.

(1) Ask the class if one thing can be in two separate places at the same time. They will deny that this is possible. Then show them two chairs, and ask the following questions:

What do these two chairs have in common? (Well, they will say, they both have arms and legs and a seat and a back.)

Okay, what do these two legs have in common; why are they both legs? (The response we often get is that "they look exactly the same"; i.e., they have the same shape.)

Okay, so let's talk about the shape that they both have. This "shape" is a Platonic Form. Does the shape exist separately from the legs?

At this point, if they want to continue to maintain that nothing can be in two different places at the same time, they will have to concede that the shape does exist separately from the legs. At the least they will revise their original view and say that they meant that a *physical thing* can't be in two separate places at the same time. This revision implicitly recognizes Forms as nonphysical "things" that can be in different places at the same time.

(2) Write "This is a philosophy class" on the board twice and ask whether there is one sentence on the board or two. After they have argued about that for a bit, you can satisfy most everyone by bringing forth the type-token distinction: The two sets of chalk marks on the board are sentence tokens, but there is one sentence type that they are tokens of. The type is a Form, and it isn't on the board, since there are two of what's on the board.

(3) This one, as we recall, comes from a text by Avrum Stroll. Ask the class to suppose that the paper on which the American Constitution is written burns up in a fire. Does that mean that America no longer has a Constitution? Nope. That's because the Constitution, a Form, exists separately from the world of physical objects.

9.	*What are the four Aristotelian causes of a baseball?*

One of our colleagues, Ric Machuga, presents the following outline to his students. He sees Aristotle as a mediating voice between the extremes of Heraclitus and Parmenides and uses that idea to present Aristotle's concept of change. The four causes of a baseball are set in their appropriate context in the outline.

Heraclitus

1.	Argued that the only source of knowledge is that which we observe through the five senses.
2.	Those senses reveal a continually changing world. A bank robber can never be charged with a crime because the person charged would be different from the person who robbed the bank originally.

Parmenides

1.	There is only one, unchanging Being;
2.	Argued that all change is illusory.
3.	If change were possible, Being would change into something else. The only thing other than Being is non-being, which (said Parmenides) amounts to nonexistence.

Aristotle

2.	Things exist
3.	Some things move and change
4.	The things in this universe that exist, move, and change are not totally unintelligible

Subject matters of the sciences (in increasing generality)

1.	Things insofar as they are able to make rational choices between competing goods (ethics)
2.	Things insofar as they are alive (biology)
3.	Things insofar as they are moving or changing objects (physics)
4.	Things insofar as they exist (metaphysics)

What is a thing?

1.	Aristotle said that things have being.
2.	The purpose of metaphysics is to make clear what being is.
3	Most things are composed of matter and form
4.	Prime matter (matter devoid of all form) is nothing more than a potential thing
5.	Pure form (form devoid of all matter) is pure actuality
6.	For Aristotle, God is pure form
7.	In most all things, however, matter and form are a unity and can only be separated conceptually

Knowing things

1. Human beings have the capacity to abstract forms from matter
2. We can observe a vast array of different objects and realize they are all trees
3. Nature is divided into natural kinds that humans discover and name when they abstract a thing's substantial form

Substantial and accidental form

1. Substantial form is that which makes a thing what it is
2. If you change a thing's substantial form, the thing becomes something else
3. Cut down an actual tree and the mass of matter is no longer a tree but is potentially either a house, firewood, or compost
4. If you change a thing's accidental form, the thing remains that kind of thing
5. We can prune a limb from a tree or pick its fruit; the accidental form of the tree changes, but the tree remains a tree

Aristotle's reply to Heraclitus

1. Our five senses reveal that the accidental forms of things are continually changing, but it is not true that a thing's substantial form is always changing
2. So while in a sense Heraclitus was correct, his radical conclusion that everything is in a continual state of flux is false

Aristotle's reply to Parmenides

1. While in a sense Parmenides was right, he fails to distinguish between actuality and potentiality and so his conclusion that nothing changes is false
2. When a thing changes its accidental form, it does not mean one thing passes out of existence to be replaced by another (different) thing
3. We may say (truthfully) that the table is white; but it is also potentially red. Painting the table does not mean the white table goes out of existence, only that the accidental form of that table changes

Cause

1. Any complete explanation of what a thing is, or why a thing changes, must mention the following four kinds of causes
2. Material cause (what makes that thing a baseball is because it is made out of cork, rubber, string, and leather)
3. Formal cause (what makes that thing a baseball is because it's in the shape of a ball)
4. Efficient cause (what makes that thing a baseball is because the maker of the ball put its parts together in a certain way)
5. Final cause (what makes that thing a baseball is because it was designed to be used in the game of baseball)

Final cause

1. According to Aristotle, an infinite series of temporal causes is impossible
2. If such an infinite series of causes existed without a first cause the series as a whole is unintelligible
3. Since Aristotle thought the universe always existed, the first cause is not temporally prior to all other causes, but it is conceptually first
4. A bowl a food causes a hungry dog to run toward it; the cause (the bowl of food) and the effect (the dog's running) exist simultaneously
5. The motion of the stars and planets (which in turn causes all other motion) must have a first cause = prime mover = God
6 For Aristotle, God is the unmoved mover, ultimately responsible as a final cause for all movement in the universe without himself moving
7. God is the unmoved mover by definition; it makes no more sense to ask "what moves God?" than it does to ask "why is a vacuum empty?"

What exists?

1. Things like rocks and people, which are sometimes moving
2. Stars and planets, which are always moving and always move other things
3. God, which always moves other things but is never himself moved

CHAPTER 4

The Philosophers of the Hellenistic and Christian Eras

Main Points

1. <u>Metaphysics in the Roman Empire</u>

   The contributions of Romans to philosophy were minimal.

2. During the Hellenistic and Roman periods there were four main traditions or "schools" of philosophy: Stoicism and Epicureanism (covered in chapter 9), and Skepticism and Neoplatonism (covered in this chapter).

3. <u>Plotinus.</u> The great philosopher of Neoplatonism found reality in unity and permanence: the One. Reality emanates from the One as light emanates from the sun; matter is the final emanation and stands on the edge of non-being. The One can be apprehended only by a coming together of the soul and the One in a mystical experience. Unlike the Christian God, Plotinus's god was not personal.

4. <u>St. Augustine.</u> Through Augustine's thought the Christian belief in an eternal and unchanging nonmaterial actuality that is the ground of all being and truth received a philosophical justification, essentially Platonic and Neoplatonic in substance. However, Augustine identified this ultimate ground not with the Forms of Plato or the nonpersonal One of Plotinus but with the Christian God.

5. Augustine accepted the Old Testament idea that God created the world *ex nihilo* (out of nothing) and the New Testament Gospel accounts of the life, death, and resurrection of Jesus Christ. Augustine believed that God took on human form in the person of Jesus, a position unthinkable for Neoplatonists who thought that the immaterial realm could not be tainted with the imperfection of mere gross matter.

6. <u>Augustine and skepticism.</u> Total skeptics maintain that nothing can be known (or profess to suspend judgment in all matters); modified skeptics do not doubt that at least some things are known, but deny or suspend judgment on the possibility of knowledge about particular things, such as God, or within some subject matter, such as history or ethics.

7. In the Hellenistic and Roman periods after Plato there were two schools of (total) skepticism, the **Pyrrhonists**, who suspended judgment on all issues, and the **Academics**, who maintained that "all things are inapprehensible."

8. **Sextus Empiricus**, a Pyrrhonist, the greatest skeptic of ancient times, set forth in Ten Tropes arguments by the ancient skeptics against the possibility of knowledge. For example, one cannot know how any object really is in itself, since what one perceives or thinks it to be is always in relationship to, never independent of, that perceiver.

9. **St. Augustine**: Skepticism is refuted by the principle of noncontradiction; by the very act of doubting—from the fact of my very doubting it follows that I am; and because sense perception itself gives a rudimentary kind of knowledge (we make no mistake if we assent to the bent appearance of a stick as it enters the water) .

10. <u>Hypatia.</u> **Hypatia of Alexandria**, a pagan, was the last major commentator on the geocentric astronomical system of Ptolemy Claudius, whose work was eventually overthrown by Nicholas Copernicus in the sixteenth century. She tried to improve the mathematics of the Ptolemaic system and tried to demonstrate the completeness of Ptolemy's astronomy. Ptolemy's work fit with the prevailing Christian theology in teaching the centrality of humankind and of the earth in God's creation.

11. Hypatia was sympathetic to Plotinus's metaphysics and to stoic philosophy. Plotinus's interpretation of Plato's metaphysics, she believed, implied a way of life, and for her, and her students, mathematics and astronomy were essential preparation for the study of metaphysics.

12. <u>The Middle Ages and Aquinas</u>

    Original philosophy was virtually nonexistent in Europe during the early Middle Ages, with the exception of Neoplatonists Boethius (sixth century) and John Scotus (ninth century).

13. Contact with the Arabian world during the high Middle Ages rekindled interest among churchmen in Aristotle.

14. The most important of those who saw accord between Christian principles and Aristotle was **St. Thomas Aquinas**, who clarified the boundary between philosophy and theology. Though a person can have true knowledge of the natural world (the kind of knowledge science produces), such knowledge is insufficient. The realm of supernatural truth, dealing with the most profound aspects of Christian belief, goes beyond human reason but is not contrary to that reason. Human reason, for example, could know that God existed and that there was but one God; but knowledge of the Trinity could come only by divine revelation. For Aquinas, philosophy is a handmaiden for theology.

15. Following Aristotle, Aquinas said that all physical things are composed of matter and form, and that the form of a thing does not exist apart from matter.

16. But Aquinas went beyond Aristotle in pointing out that *what* something is is not the same as *that* it is (its existence). Existence is the most important actuality in anything, without which even *what* something is (its form) cannot be actual.

17. Aquinas also emphasized that nothing could cause its own existence and must be caused to exist by something already existing, and, ultimately, by the Uncaused Cause of Existence (God). Aquinas went beyond Aristotle's conception of God as Pure Act (because God is changeless) to an understanding of God as Pure Act of Existence.

18. For Aquinas, the "essential form" of the human body is the soul. The soul is pure form without matter and as such is immortal. Each soul is a direct creation of God and does not come from human parents. It stands in a relationship of mutual interdependency relative to the body. A human being is a unity of body and soul. Without the soul the body would be formless; without a body the soul would have no access to knowledge derived from sensation.

19. Aquinas's epistemology was built on Aristotle's notion of three powers of the soul: the vegetative (e.g., reproduction), animal (e.g., sensation), and human (e.g., the understanding). Knowledge is reached when the picture in the understanding agrees with what is present in reality. This knowledge is empirical in that it comes from the senses, but human imagination and intelligence are required to discover the essence of things that represents their definition.

20. Aquinas's proofs for God's existence rely on the idea that things must have an ultimate cause, creator, designer, source of being, or source of goodness (i.e., God). But our knowledge of God's nature is in terms of what God is not—unmoved and unchangeable (eternal), not material and without parts (utterly simple), not a composite (God's essence is his existence).

21. Aquinas believed that the task of the wise person is to find both order and reason in the natural world. Interest in Aquinas experienced a strong revival in the nineteenth and twentieth centuries.

Boxes

- Plotinus

- Profile: St. Augustine

- Augustine, God, and Time
  (Augustine's analysis of time)

- Pyrrho
  (Mentions also epoche, ataraxia, and agoge)

- Sextus's Asterisk
  (Sextus maneuvers around some possible criticism by not counting "involuntary judgments" as knowledge-claims)

- Profile: Hypatia of Alexandria

- Universals
  (The "problem of universals" and the answers given by realism, conceptualism, and nominalism)

- Teleological Explanations
  (Teleological and modern causal explanations compared. [Note that explanations of an organism's characteristics in terms of natural selection and evolution may seem teleological, but this is superficial appearance only])

Readings

4.1   St. Augustine, from *Confessions*

Augustine on time and eternity.

Philosophers' Principal Works

- Pyrrho of Elis (c. 365–270 B.C.)

- Diogenes Laertius (c. A.D. 200)
  Lives and Opinions of the Eminent Philosophers

- Plotinus (c. 204–270)
  Enneads

- Sextus Empiricus (third century)
  Outlines of Pyrrhonism
  Against the Dogmatists
  Hypotoposes

- Augustine (354–430)
  Confessions
  De Genesi ad Litteram
  De Trinitate
  The City of God

- Hypatia (c. 370/75–415)

- Thomas Aquinas (1225–1274)
  On Being and Essence (1253)
  Truth (Quaestiones Disputatae de Veritate [1256–1259])
  Summa contra Gentiles (1258–1260)
  On the Power of God (1265)
  Summa Theologica (1265–1269)
  In Librum de Causis (1271)

Lecture-Discussion Ideas Related to Selected Questions

4. *Defend some version of total skepticism.*

One of Peter Unger's arguments in *Ignorance: A Case for Scepticism* (Oxford: Clarendon Press, 1975) can be counted on to stimulate a good discussion among beginning philosophy students. Basically Unger's argument, to paraphrase, is this: No one is certain of anything; therefore, since you can know something to be so only if you are certain of it, you cannot know anything.

What makes the argument interesting is, among other things, Unger's reason for maintaining the first premise, that no one is certain of anything. "Certain," he says, is an absolute term like "flat." If a surface is flat, then no surface can ever be flatter. Likewise, "if someone is certain of something then there never is anything of which he or anyone else is more certain. . . . Thus, if it is logically possible that there be something of which any person might be more certain than he now is of a given thing (as there always is), then he is not actually certain of that thing."

It is because of the absolute nature of "certain" that the first premise supposedly holds.

The argument certainly is not beyond criticism.

8.   *Can we say only what God is not?*

No, of course not. God is good, God is caring, God is loving, etc., etc. But the thing is, what do we *mean* when we say that God is good, caring, and so on? Skeptics argue that such positive descriptions of God either are meaningless honorific phrases or can only be clarified by resorting to further negative descriptions.

The fundamental problem, we think, is this: the predicates that we apply to God connote temporality, but God, according to the most popular conceptions of God, is not in time. So what can these predications mean? What is nontemporal caring and loving? Or is there some way that God's caring can be in time while God himself is not in time?

Aquinas's treatment of the analogical nature of religious language is in Question XIII of Part I of *Summa Theologica.*

CHAPTER 5

The Modern Period

Main Points

1. Historical developments after the Renaissance, especially the growth of science, led to the shaping of metaphysics and epistemology, including the commonsense view of today that reality has a dual nature of physical objects and mind.

2. Important (and conflicting) metaphysical perspectives: dualism (what exists is either physical or mental, or, in the case of human beings, some combination of both); materialism or physicalism (only the physical exists); idealism (only the mental or spiritual exists); a "neither-nor" view (what exists is ultimately neither mental nor physical); double aspect theory (what exists is ultimately both mental and physical—the mental and physical are just different ways of looking at the same things, which in themselves are neutral between the two categories).

3. Modern metaphysics is largely an attempt to ascertain the validity of each of these positions.

4. Descartes and Dualism

   Descartes began modern philosophy and in metaphysics employed skepticism to arrive (he thought) at truth and knowledge. If anything is beyond doubt, it can provide a criterion of truth and knowledge.

5. Skepticism as the key to certainty. Two famous conjectures he employed were the dream conjecture and the evil demon conjecture.

6. He could doubt at first everything except the truth expressed in *"cogito, ergo sum."*

7. <u>The "clear and distinct" litmus test.</u> From *cogito, ergo sum* Descartes worked his way to the clear and distinct criterion of truth: anything that was as clear and distinct as his own existence would pass the litmus test and would also have to be certain. This doubting methodology was like geometry, using as an axiom "I think, therefore I am" to prove true what at first only seemed true.

8. Using the "clear and distinct" criterion, Descartes found that he had a certain knowledge of God's existence and, from knowledge that God would not deceive him, Descartes concluded that he also had certain knowledge that there existed a world of objects outside his mind.

9. The essential attribute of material substance is extension (occupancy of space); the essential attribute of mind is thought. Mind and matter are totally independent of each other.

10. Difficulties in dualism include reconciling the belief that material things are completely subject to physical laws with the belief that the immaterial mind can move one's body.

11. Descartes took an epistemological detour in trying to discover metaphysical truth about what is through epistemological inquiry about what can be known.

12. **Hobbes** in his natural philosophy thought that all that exists is bodies in motion, this being true not only of what ordinarily is viewed as physical bodies but also of mind and emotion.

13. That is, all mental phenomena derive from perception, i.e., "sense." Thus, Hobbes espoused materialism.

14. <u>Hobbes and Materialism</u>

    <u>Perception.</u> All mental phenomena are derived from perception, which is itself nothing but "matter in motion." Motions outside us cause motions within us. Hobbes tried to establish that every aspect of human psychology, including memory and imagination, thought, reasoning, and decision making, are all a product of perception.

15. <u>Difficulties.</u> Hobbes's materialist psychology encounters difficulties in explaining perception. The perception of a green and soft lawn is not itself green and soft, but is nothing more than the movement of particles. How is the movement of particles experienced as green and soft, and what is it that has those experiences?

16. <u>Spinoza and Conway</u>

    <u>Anne Conway.</u> A forerunner of Leibniz's monadology, Lady Conway's view was that all things are reducible to a single substance that is itself irreducible, but there is a continuum between material and mental substances so that all created substances are both mental and physical to some degree or other.

17. All "Creatures" (i.e., created substances) are dependent on God's decision to create them. All such creatures have an individual essence and an essence common to all. The latter came to be known as *de re* modality—meaning that a property (in this case, the property of being both mental and physical) must be a property of anything that is created by God. Everything (other than God) is a substance and must of necessity exist as partly physical and partly mental.

18. Conway's God is nonmaterial, nonphysical, all-perfect, and exists outside the dimension of time. God is the eternal creator; the universe has always existed because God has always existed and he has always been creating.

19. Spinoza. He regarded thought and extension as different attributes of one basic substance equated with God. A living person is not the composite of mind and matter, but rather a "modification" of the one substance. The mind and body are the same thing, conceptualized from different viewpoints. Thus, there is no problem explaining how the mind interacts with the body: they are one and the same thing.

20. Spinoza was a pantheist: God is all. There is no personal immortality after death, and free will is an illusion.

21. Though both Hobbes and Spinoza believed there was only one substance, Hobbes had the problem of explaining away the mental.

22. John Locke, Berkeley, and Idealism

    Representative Realism. Locke's fundamental thesis is that all our ideas come from experience and that the human mind at birth is a *tabula rasa* (blank slate).

23. *Nihil in intellectu quod prius non fuerit in sensu* ("nothing exists in the mind that was not first in the senses").

24. **Locke's** representative realism—we perceive objects indirectly by our ideas or representations of them—is now thought to be so much common sense.

25. George Berkeley. If representative realism is correct, Berkeley argued, then we cannot know that any of our ideas or perceptions accurately represent the qualities of sensible things since we cannot compare the ideas we have of an object with the object itself. We do not experience the object itself but only our perceptions or ideas of the object.

26. The objects of human knowledge consist of "ideas" (1) conveyed to the mind by the senses, (2) perceived by the mind when the mind reflects on its own operations, or (3) compounded or divided by the mind with the help of memory or imagination. What exists, therefore, are ideas and the minds that have them. It is contradictory to suppose that material substances exist outside the mind that perceives them.

27. *Esse est percipi* ("to be is to be perceived").

28. If secondary qualities (e.g., tastes, odors, colors) exist only in the mind, then so do primary qualities (e.g., extension, figure, motion) since they are all relative to the observer.

29. Material things as clusters of ideas. Berkeley's view is one version of idealism. He maintains that sensible things are not material things that exist outside the mind but are directly perceived clusters of ideas within the mind.

30. Berkeley believed that the perceiving mind of God makes possible the continued existence of sensible things when we are not perceiving them.

31. Commonsense objections that Berkeley's idealism renders the physical world intangible or imaginary are based on a misunderstanding of Berkeley.

Boxes

- The Scientific Revolution
  (Copernicus ushers in a new era of discovery and a new worldview)

- Chronology of Postmedieval History

- Profile: René Descartes

- Descartes's Conjectures
  (Descartes's two skeptical conjectures explained)

- Variations on a Theme
  (The theme being "I think, therefore I exist.")

- Parallelism
  (According to this "explanation," the mind and body only appear to interact)

- God, Free Will, Immortality
  (It's the existence of these three things that is at stake in modern metaphysics)

- Profile: Anne Finch, The Viscountess Conway

- Profile: Benedictus de Spinoza

- Leibniz
  (A brief look at Leibniz's monads with a mention of the plausible assumptions on which he based his metaphysics: the principle of the identity of indiscernibles and the principle of sufficient reason)

- Profile: Émilie du Châtelet

- Profile: George Berkeley

- Rationalism and Empiricism
  (An important box on the difference between the two)

- Berkeley and Atheism
  (Berkeley believed that dualism and materialism lead to skepticism)

- Berkeley's Proofs of God
  (They might have gone in Part 3, Philosophy of Religion, but we thought they fit better here)

- Berkeley's Argument Analyzed
  (Have students try to refute the argument stated in this box)

Readings

5.1   René Descartes, from *Meditations on First Philosophy*

The excerpt contains both of Descartes's skeptical conjectures and his explanation that he is a thinking thing—a mind—a thing that is one and indivisible but is intermingled with something entirely different, a body—something that is divisible and has parts.

5.2   George Berkeley, from *Treatise Concerning the Principles of Human Knowledge*

Berkeley notes that the objects of human knowledge are ideas and that these ideas can only exist in the mind that perceives them. He then observes that there is a contradiction in the view that sensible objects exist outside the mind. He goes on to argue that all the qualities we experience when we experience a sensible object (not just the so-called secondary qualities) are ideas that exist in the mind and that the existence of things outside the mind cannot be proven by reason; in fact, Berkeley argues, it is impossible even to conceive of a sensible thing existing outside the mind.

Philosophers' Principal Works

- René Descartes (1596–1650)
  Discourse on Method (1637)
  Meditations on First Philosophy (1641)
  Principles of Philosophy (1644)

- Thomas Hobbes (1588–1679)
  De Cive (1642)
  De Corpore Politico (1650)
  Leviathan (1651)
  The Questions Concerning Liberty, Necessity, and Chance (1656)
  De Corpore (1665)
  Behemoth (1682)

- Anne Finch, The Viscountess Conway (1631–1679)
  The Principles of the Most Ancient and Modern Philosophy (1671–1674? 1677–1679?)

- Benedictus de Spinoza (1632–1677)
  Ethics (probably finished 1665; published 1677)
  Tractatus Theologico-politicus (1670)

- John Locke (1632–1704)
  An Essay Concerning Human Understanding (1689)
  Two Treatises of Government (1690)

- George Berkeley (1685–1753)
  Essay Towards a New Theory of Vision (1709)
  A Treatise Concerning the Principles of Human Knowledge (1710)
  Three Dialogues Between Hylas and Philonous (1713)

- Gottfried Wilhelm, Baron von Leibniz (1646–1716)
  The Theodicy (1710)
  Monadology (1714)

- Émilie du Châtelet (1707–1749)
  Institutions de Physique (1740)

Lecture-Discussion Ideas Related to Selected Questions

5. *"Material things, including one's own body, are completely subject to physical laws." "The immaterial mind can move one's body." Are these two claims incompatible? Explain.*

It's dead certain that your class will accept both these ideas. They really should be aware of the problems.

Can the body be subject to physical laws while being moved by something that is nonphysical?

Perhaps, but there is this difficulty: if a nonphysical something moves the body but only in such a way that the body is always subject to physical laws, then the nonphysical something seems eliminable by Ockham's razor. A car analogy may be useful: When you depress the gas pedal the pistons move faster and the crankshaft rotates faster and the wheels turn faster and it all happens in accordance with the principles of internal combustion engine mechanics. Maybe something nonphysical causes the pistons to move faster and the crankshaft and wheels to turn faster when the gas pedal is depressed, but why suppose this?

Further, if the immaterial mind's moving the body entails that a person could have acted differently in the same circumstances, there is this difficulty: if the person could have acted differently in the same circumstances, then his or her body could have moved differently in the same circumstances. But if a physical thing could have moved differently in the same circumstances, it is not governed by physical laws.

Various suggestions have been made as to how a nonphysical mind might interact with a body that (presumably) nevertheless is completely subject to physical laws, and one of them might be discussed. The most famous of the lot is probably John Eccles (with Karl Popper), *The Self and Its Brain* (New York: Springer International, 1977).

Eccles theorizes, in effect, that the mind (not his word) may affect the patterns of discharge of neuron populations in the brain. The trouble with this is that nothing that happens in the brain seems to require the nonphysical mind as its explanation and it does not seem possible either to confirm or to disconfirm Eccles's theory. The theory, in short, seems gratuitous. One of us discussed this elsewhere, briefly: see Brooke Noel Moore, *The Philosophical Possibilities Beyond Death* (Springfield: Charles C Thomas, 1981).

14.   Do *we have knowledge of external objects? Explain.*

Rather than provide a general answer to this question, we want to focus on a subsidiary question: Could the universe exist even in the absence of thought about it?

We hear a lot these days to the effect that contemporary astrophysics lends support to idealism through something called the anthropic principle. We cannot help you very much with this principle, but we would like to make you aware of it, in case you are not.

There are evidently at least two versions of this principle, a weak version and a strong version.

A weak version, as set forth by Brandon Carter, is that a complete account of the universe must explain the fact that the universe contains observers. A stronger version is that the universe must have such properties as to admit observers to exist in it at some stage in its development. This is sometimes expressed by saying that the constants and laws of nature must be such that life can exist.

A very strong version of the principle, associated with the physicist J. A. Wheeler, is to the effect that the production of observers at some stage in the universe is essential to bringing it into being. Proponents of this very strong version, if we understand them correctly, theorize that the universe acquires reality back to its beginning in the Big Bang only when after eons it brings about observership. The theory is illustrated by the "double-slit" experiment, in which the experimenter decides, *after* a photon has passed through a screen with two slits, whether it *will* pass through both slits or only one. The experimenter makes this decision by opening or closing a venetian blind beyond the screen *after* the photon has already passed through the screen but *before* it reaches the blind. If he opens the blind, he records through which slit the photon passes; whereas if he closes it and uses it for a photographic plate, the interference pattern reveals that the photon went through both slits. In the first instance the photon behaves as a particle, and in the second its behavior is wavelike. Similarly, it is theorized, the reality of the universe in the Big Bang and since is dependent on the occurrence of observers now.

We do not really feel competent to comment on the experiment or on its application to the very strong anthropic principle. If you want to pursue the subject, see John D. Barrow and Frank J. Tipler, *The Anthropic Cosmological Principle* (Oxford: Clarendon, 1986). This much at least can be said: the first two versions stated above certainly are not equivalent to idealism. The third version also is not equivalent to idealism, though it certainly assigns an importance to observation that exceeds that suggested by common sense; and in any case seems to be pretty speculative at this point.

19.   *Psychokinesis is the mental power by which psychics claim to make changes in the external physical world—to bend spoons, to cause balls to roll, and so on. Is there any difference between using your mind to bend a spoon and using your mind to bend your arm? Explain.*

We think there is no difference, and we think that our students should recognize this, because it will help them appreciate that ordinary, everyday mind-body interaction is a pretty mysterious business, if you think the mind is nonmaterial. (You may disagree with us on these points.)

It only seems as if there is a difference because there is direct physiological linkage between a psychic's arm and brain, whereas (assuming that there is psychokinesis) any balls the psychic causes to roll or spoons he or she causes to bend through "psychokinesis" are not linked with his or her brain. So psychics seem to be much "closer" to their arms than to the balls and spoons they manipulate through psychokinesis.

Of course, if the mind *is* the brain, then the psychic's arm, unlike the balls and spoons, really is linked to his or her mind. But if the mind is *nonphysical*, then the psychic's arm is no closer to his or her mind than are the spoons and balls. If the mind is nonphysical, then the mind's moving an arm (or causing brain neurons to fire) is no more mysterious than psychokinesis. In fact, it *is* psychokinesis.

And that means that any skepticism someone has about psychokinesis should be equally felt relative to the idea that the nonmaterial mind causes the limbs to move.

It's too bad you can't move a ball with psychokinesis to add a little color to the discussion (if you can, we'd like to hear from you). What you can do is point out that, if you were to give a demonstration of psychokinesis, everyone in the class would suspect a trick. So shouldn't they respond with the same skepticism when you claim that you used your immaterial mind to raise your arm?

CHAPTER 6

The Eighteenth and Nineteenth Centuries

Main Points

1.   <u>David Hume</u>

     Hume believed that knowledge is limited to what is experienced; i.e., sensory impressions. Though he displays total skepticism in some passages, in most he appears to be a modified skeptic who focuses on the nature of the self, causality, induction, God, and the external world.

2.   **Hume's** epistemology rested on four assumptions: (1) Thought, knowledge, belief, conception, judgment consist in having ideas (2) all of which are copies of impressions of sense or of inner feelings. (3) Every claim that something exists is a factual claim, and (4) factual claims can be established only by observation or by causal inference from what is observed.

3.   <u>The quarter experiment.</u> "The only existences, of which we are certain, are perceptions." Hume held, in his *A Treatise of Human Nature*, that we may observe a conjunction or relation of cause and effect only between different perceptions and can never observe it between perceptions and objects. Therefore, from the existence of perceptions we can never form any conclusion concerning the existence of objects.

4.   <u>Hume on the self.</u> We have no experience of the self or mind, supposedly an unchanging nonmaterial substance within us.

5.   Hume on cause and effect. We have no experience of a necessary connection between cause and effect; and even after we observe a frequent and constant conjunction between a cause and its effect there is no rational justification for supposing that that conjunction will repeat itself in the future.

6.   Hume: All reasoning based on present and past experience rests on the unprovable assumption that the future will resemble the past: all inferences from experience are only suppositions. This leads to total skepticism.

7.   Immanuel Kant

Kant believed that knowledge that was certain does exist and tried to show how this could be possible given Hume's arguments that indicate the opposite.

8.   The ordering principles of the mind. Kant said that knowledge begins with experience but does not all arise from experience.

9.   Kant: The constituents of experience must always be ordered and organized in certain ways even to qualify as experience; and it is possible to have knowledge of the underlying principles in terms of which the constituents of experience are ordered.

10. Perceptions must be conceptualized and unified. Perceptions must be organized under concepts for genuine experience to occur; and in one consciousness; and conceptualization and unification must conform to spatial-temporal shaping and to cause-effect relationships.

11. Kant: We thus have certain knowledge that experienceable objects are in space and time, stand in causal relationships with one another, and must conform to other rules of the understanding: they must conform because if they did not they could not qualify as experience.

12. Things-in-themselves. But we cannot say that things as they are in themselves, as they are independently of experience, must also conform to these principles and rules. Skepticism is unavoidable as to things-in-themselves.

13. The Nineteenth Century

Response to Kant's epistemology was absolute idealism, the philosophies of Fichte, Schelling, **Hegel**. Whatever is, they said, is knowable; therefore thought doesn't merely categorize reality, its categories are reality. There cannot be unknowable things in themselves, for everything is the product of the knowing mind.

14. **Hegel**, the most important of the German idealists, thought that the categories of thought are the categories of being. He held that the cosmos and its history are the concrete expression of infinite or absolute thought.

15. <u>Main themes of Hegel.</u> (1) What is most real (the Absolute) is thought thinking of itself; (2) the objective world is an unfolding or expression of infinite thought; (3) reality is an integrated whole in which each proposition (each state of affairs) is logically connected with all the rest; (4) the Absolute (the sum total of reality) is a system of conceptual triads (thesis, antithesis, synthesis).

16. Nature and Idea, as thesis and antithesis, have their synthesis in what Hegel called Spirit ("thought knowing itself both as thought and as object"). The philosophy of Spirit has three main subdivisions: subjective spirit (thesis, the realm of the human mind), objective spirit (antithesis, the mind in external manifestations in social institutions), and Absolute Spirit (synthesis).

17. Hegel's all-inclusive system represents the towering summit of metaphysical speculation.

18. <u>Reactions: Kierkegaard, Schopenhauer, and Nietzsche.</u> **Kierkegaard**, scornful of Hegel's grandiose scheme, began the existentialist tradition that is entirely concerned with how and what to choose in the face of doubt and uncertainty.

19. **Schopenhauer** famously attacked Hegel's exuberant rationalism. Schopenhauer regarded all phenomena as the objectification of the will. Will-in-itself is the originating source of everything that happens and is not determined by anything else. Blind and purposeless, will-in-itself manifests itself in the constant striving of human beings. The world is in disarray because persons are witless lackeys of this errant, cosmic will.

20. Peace can only be achieved by escaping the tyranny of the will, by moving beyond knowledge of one's own will to objectivity and understanding of will-in-itself, in which state the world of phenomena becomes a kind of nothingness. This detached state of ecstasy and rapture could be glimpsed through art, music, and aesthetic experience.

21. Schopenhauer's views influenced the psychoanalytic theories of **Sigmund Freud.**

22. **Nietzsche** rejected Hegel's Idealism but disagreed with Schopenhauer in maintaining that the world was driven and determined by the will to power. The Superman embraces the will to power and overthrows the submissive and mediocre "slave" morality that permeates society and dominates religion.

23. Nietzsche: The Superman creates rather than discovers values. God is dead.

24. Nietzsche: There are no facts, only interpretations; his philosophy was consciously antimetaphysical, though he did subscribe to the metaphysical concept of "the eternal recurrence of the same."

25. <u>John Stuart Mill.</u> Unfazed by Kant, Mill accepted the basic empiricist premise of Locke, Berkeley, and Hume that all knowledge derives from sense experience alone.

26. Mill: What we commonly deem a thing outside us; for example, a table is a permanent possibility of sensation.

27. Mill: Is the mind a permanent possibility of experience (of awareness)? He was doubtful because the mind sometimes is aware of its own awareness.

Boxes

- Profile: David Hume

- A Lot of Destruction
  (Sydney Smith's little witticism about Berkeley and Hume)

- Hume As a Total Skeptic
  (A total skeptic doubts his doubts)

- Profile: Immanuel Kant

- The Copernican Revolution in Philosophy
  (Explains what Kant called his most fundamental epistemological insight)

- Ding-an-sich
  (Includes Kant's distinction between phenomena and noumena)

- Profile: Georg Hegel

- Profile: Søren Kierkegaard

- Profile: Friedrich Wilhelm Nietzsche

- Profile: John Stuart Mill

Readings

6.1   David Hume, from *An Inquiry Concerning Human Understanding*

If experience is the foundation of all our reasoning about matters of fact, then the foundation on which we base our notions of cause and effect, and inference from past events to future prospects, is shaky indeed.

6.2   Immanuel Kant, from *Critique of Pure Reason*

Kant's metaphysical exposition of the concept of time with his conclusion that "Time is the formal *a priori* condition of all appearances whatsoever."

6.3   Georg Hegel, from *The Philosophy of History*

Hegel asserts that reason is that by which and in which all reality has its being and subsistence. No argument is presented in this passage, but it is a nice, clear statement of the basic Hegelian thesis.

6.4   Arthur Schopenhauer, from *The World As Will and Representation*

Schopenhauer's case for idealism, and argument against the notion that the world can be explained most fundamentally in terms of matter or intellect. He concludes that "the world, as we know it, exists only for our knowledge, and consequently in the *representation* alone. . . . the thing-in-itself, in other words, that which exists independently of our knowledge and of all knowledge, is to be regarded as something quite different from the *representation* and all its attributes, and hence from objectivity in general." But Schopenhauer goes on to assert that "the intellect and mater are correlatives. . . . They are in fact really one and the same thing, considered from two opposite points of view; and this one thing . . . is the phenomenon of the will or of the thing-in-itself. Consequently, both are secondary, and therefore the origin of the world is not to be looked for in either of them."

Philosophers' Principal Works

- David Hume (1711–1776)
  A Treatise of Human Nature (1739–1740)
  An Enquiry Concerning Human Understanding (1748)
  An Enquiry Concerning the Principles of Morals (1751)
  Dialogues Concerning Natural Religion (1779)

- Immanuel Kant (1724–1804)
  Critique of Pure Reason (1781)
  Prolegomena to Any Future Metaphysics (1783)
  Foundations of the Metaphysics of Morals (1785)
  Critique of Practical Reason (1788)
  Critique of Judgment (1790)

- Friedrich Wilhelm Joseph von Schelling (1775–1854)
  System of Transcendental Idealism (1807)
  The Philosophy of Art (1845)
  Of Human Freedom (trans. 1936)
  The Ages of the World (trans. 1942)

- Johann Gottlieb Fichte (1762–1814)
  The Science of Ethics as Based on the Science of Knowledge (1798)
  Critique of All Revelation (1792)
  The Characteristics of the Present Age (1806)
  The Science of Knowledge (trans. 1868)

- Georg Wilhelm Friedrich Hegel (1780–1831)
  Phenomenology of Mind (1807)
  Science of Logic (1812–1816)
  Encyclopedia of the Philosophical Sciences (1817)
  Philosophy of Right (1821)

- Arthur Schopenhauer (1788–1860)
  The World as Will and Representation (1818)
  The Basis of Morality (1841)
  "The Fourfold Root of the Principle of Sufficient Reason" (trans. 1888)

- Sigmund Freud (1856–1939)
  The Interpretation of Dreams (1900)
  Three Essays on the Theory of Sexuality (1905)
  Beyond the Pleasure Principle (1920)
  The Future of an Illusion (1927)
  Civilization and Its Discontents (1930)
  An Outline of Psychoanalysis (1939)

- Søren Kierkegaard (1813–1855)
  Either/Or (1843)
  Philosophical Fragments (1844)
  The Concluding Unscientific Postscript (1846)

- Friedrich Nietzsche (1849–1900)
  The Birth of Tragedy (1872)
  Beyond Good and Evil (1886)
  Twilight of the Idols (1888)
  Ecce Home (1888)
  Thus Spoke Zarathustra (1883–1891)

- John Stuart Mill (1806–1873)
  A System of Logic (1843)
  On Liberty (1859)
  Utilitarianism (1863)
  Autobiography (1867)
  The Subjection of Women (1869)

Lecture-Discussion Ideas Related to Selected Questions

1.   *Do you ever observe anything other than your own perceptions? Explain.*

As related to this question we should not forget Kant's "Refutation of Idealism," which appears in the second (B) edition of Kant's *Critique of Pure Reason* (B 274). According to Kant, the Refutation proves that "we have experience of outer things" and shows that "inner experience in general is possible only through outer experience in general." Our students have responded quite favorably to discussions of Kant's Refutation.

The Refutation contains more than one line of argument, but the main one is to the effect that your consciousness of your own existence as in time presupposes perception of "something permanent" (i.e., something more permanent than individual perceptions themselves), and that this perception of a permanent is possible only through actual things outside you (and not just mere ideas of such things).

Here is a paraphrase of Kant's thinking that has worked well for us in introductory classes. It will reflect the influence of Strawson, Bennett, Wilkerson, Gram, Paton, and others.

1.   I am aware of my experience as in time, as a succession of momentary items that are related temporally to one another.

2.   Awareness of my experiences as in time presupposes something permanent, a system of reidentifiable things that last longer than my momentary experiences. (Here see Kant's "first analogy of experience.")

3.   The "something permanent" cannot be something within my experiences, because they are all momentary items, the temporal relationships among which are apprehended only by reference to something beyond themselves.

4.   So the permanent (which must be perceived for me to be aware of the temporality of my experiences) is possible only through the existence of things outside me, and not through the mere idea of things outside me.

5.   So awareness of my own existence as determined in time is possible only through the existence of things outside me (and hence in space).

In other words, awareness of the succession of my ideas is possible only through the existence of permanent things (reidentifiable particulars) that I perceive outside me.

The argument is very slippery, and it goes without saying that many remain unconvinced.

8.   *Do infants have experience? Do cats? Fish? Explain.*

Not all of our students say that infants alone on the list qualify as at some stage or another having *experience*. The operative word here, of course, is "experience," and the question is just simply a device to get students to think about some of the necessary ingredients of experience. They aren't likely to have done so ever before.

Kant, whose *Critique of Pure Reason* is largely just a large-scale (and brilliant) analysis of the concept of experience, would say that several conditions must be met before a mere sentience shades up into experience, and these alleged conditions might profitably be discussed with a class of beginning students. If they don't get anything else from the discussion, they are likely to get an appreciation of the insight of Kant and of philosophers in general.

Among the Kantian conditions we think there are two that are especially fruitful to discuss in an introductory course:

1. Experience requires that the data of sensation be recognized; that is, that particular things be *categorized* as being such-and-such *kind* of thing. A mere stream of awarenesses or sensory particulars does not qualify as experience without this recognition.

2. Experience also requires potential self-ascription of sensation, awareness of the data of sensation as belonging to a subject that has the awareness.

Kant, of course, maintained that experience requires other things, notably that the particulars of sensation be perceived as in space and time and be apprehended in terms of his list of categories; and he also argued that you cannot have experience unless there actually exists an external world. The validity of these ideas has been challenged, of course. Introductory classes might not be prepared to evaluate them critically, though they certainly can understand them.

While we're on the subject of experience, it might be of interest to pose the following question to your students. Some of our comments below anticipate the discussion in chapter 8 on the philosophy of mind.

Can two different people ever have the identical experience? That is, can the experience of one person ever simultaneously be the experience of another person? Why or why not?

Here is Juan and there is Juanita. Juan and Juanita both experienced the San Francisco earthquake of 1989. So they both had the same experience. That is to say, they both had qualitatively identical experiences. But they did not, and could not, have numerically identical experiences. Juan's experience counts as one experience and Juanita's experience counts as one experience, and one and one make two experiences. When it comes to counting the experiences of different people, we abide by the rule that numerically the selfsame experience cannot be had by two or more people.

The *materialist* won't allow violation of this rule and admit that two people could have the same experience because, since an experience happens at some place and time, two people, being physical things, cannot simultaneously occupy exactly the same space.

The *nonmaterialist who believes that mind-body dependency entails that the body cannot have experience except through the body's sensory apparatus* won't allow violation of the rule for the same reason.

The *nonmaterialist who believes that disembodied minds/persons are possible* won't allow violation of the rule even though this type of nonphysicalist apparently is not required to think of an experience as happening at a place.

Such a nonmaterialist won't allow violation of the rule because if two minds/persons could have the same experience, then it would not be clear how minds/persons could be individuated: what would be the difference between a single mind/person that had one experience and two minds/persons that had shared an experience?

Some (admittedly farfetched) counterexamples to the rule (the selfsame experience cannot be had by two or more people) that a beginning philosophy class might find interesting to consider are these:

1. Suppose Juan and Juanita communicate through ESP: Juan is able to "read Juanita's mind." Assuming that he can, when he does is it a case of two people having the selfsame experience?

2. Suppose Juan's body has been replicated through a Star Trek procedure. If the replication is faithful, then everything Juan remembers (prior to the replication), Juan-replica will also remember. So, if Juan remembers the San Francisco earthquake, so will Juan-replica. Is this a case of two persons having the selfsame experience, in this case a memory?

3. Suppose Juan and Juanita do not each have a brain. Instead, thanks to Star Trek technology, they share a common brain that is housed in a lab somewhere and to which they are connected by synthetic nerve tissue, analogously to computer terminals connected to a central processing unit and active memory. Couldn't Juan and Juanita have the selfsame experiences?

4. Suppose Juan and Juanita are the Jekyll and Hyde personalities manifested by the same individual. Multiple personalities are often thought of as separate persons. Couldn't the selfsame experience be the experience of Juan and then later, when Juanita took over, the experience of Juanita?

Our view is that none of these truly are counterexamples to the rule that two people cannot have numerically the selfsame experience. Maybe you won't agree.

CHAPTER 7

The Continental Tradition

Main Points

1. Much of what happened in Western philosophy after Hegel was in response to Hegel. Analytic philosophy became the predominant tradition in England and eventually the United States (where pragmatism also developed). What is called Continental philosophy developed on the European continent.

2. Continental philosophy includes existentialism, phenomenology, hermeneutics, deconstruction, and critical theory. The most influential schools, existentialism and phenomenology, are covered in this chapter; the others will be covered in chapter 13.

3. Existentialism

   Kierkegaard and Nietzsche are important forerunners of existentialism. Both held that philosophical systems that seek to make everything seem rational fail because not everything is. They are futile attempts to overcome pessimism and despair.

4. **Kierkegaard** opposed the Hegelian view of the world's utterly rationality.

5. Philosophy must speak to anguished existence in an irrational world, and Kierkegaard viewed with disdain philosophy's concern with ideal truths and abstract metaphysics. The earth is a place of suffering, fear, and dread. The central philosophical problem is *sickness-unto-death*; only subjective commitment to God can grant relief.

6. **Schopenhauer** also looked at Hegel's philosophy of absolute reason unfavorably (indeed, contemptuously). He viewed humanity as mostly irrational, driven by selfishness, base desires.

7. **Nietzsche** further developed this critique of rationalist idealism.

8. Nietzsche: People have become enslaved by a slave morality that rejects life, celebrates mediocrity, and renders people cowardly, reactionary, and lacking in purpose.

9. The concern for the situation of the individual person, denial of the rationality of the world, awareness of the vacuousness and triviality of human existence, and the attempts to find the answer to despair spread into arts, literature, and culture generally (as found, for instance, in Dadaism, Surrealism, Expressionism, Freud, Kafka, Ionesco, Beckett, and Bergman), and persist in philosophy.

10. Some of whose main themes in existentialism are: (1) Traditional and academic philosophy is sterile and remote from real life; (2) Philosophy must focus on the individual in his or her confrontation with the world; (3) The world is irrational, beyond total comprehension or accurate philosophical conceptualization; (4) The world is absurd: there is no explanation why it is the way it is; (5) Senselessness, triviality, separation, and so on, pervade human existence causing anxiety, dread, self-doubt, and despair; (6) One faces the necessity of choosing how to live within this absurd and irrational world. This is the *existential predicament*.

11. <u>Two Existentialists</u>

    Existentialism as a philosophical movement was something of a direct response to social ills; Albert Camus and Jean-Paul Sartre wrote drama, novels, and political tracts, as well as philosophical works.

12. <u>Albert Camus.</u> **Camus**: We mask despair in an absurd world with false optimism and self-deception. We are strangers to ourselves.

13. The world defeats our most fundamental needs. When we see this, the basic question is, Is there any reason not to commit suicide? Yet suicide is an unacceptable acquiescence. Only by struggling against the absurdity of life is it possible to give life meaning and value. The fate of Sisyphus illustrates life.

14. Camus increasingly focused his concern on the inhumanity and cruelty of the world. The individual must spend life fighting the "plague" of injustice and violence through measured and nonfanatical revolt.

15. <u>Jean-Paul Sartre.</u> Camus was agnostic. **Sartre** was atheistic.

16. Sartre: Man is abandoned; that is, God does not exist.

17. Implications of abandonment: (1) There is no common human nature or essence; existence precedes essence; you are what you make of yourself; (2) There is no ultimate reason why things are the way they are and not some other way; (3) Because there is no divine plan there is no determinism: man is free; (4) There is no objective standard of values.

18. Hence, we are responsible for what we are and must choose our own values. And in doing so we choose for all.

19. We experience our responsibility in anguish or hide from it in bad faith. Only through acceptance of our responsibility and in choosing a fundamental life project may we live in authenticity.

20. Phenomenology

    Husserl, the first great phenomenologist, proposed to establish a new foundation for human knowing: a universal phenomenology of consciousness, whose purpose is to investigate phenomena while "bracketing" assumptions and presuppositions about the world, so as to reveal what is certain in consciousness.

21. Husserl accepted Brentano's idea that consciousness is intentional.

22. Husserl: Philosophy must return to "the things themselves," the objects disclosed in conscious experience by phenomenological analysis.

23. Martin Heidegger. For **Heidegger** the truth of things lies not in phenomena but in Being itself. Being itself has been reduced to a world of objects (i.e., it has been forgotten).

24. We are basically ignorant about the thing that matters most: the true nature of Being. Awareness of the priority of Being would require a new beginning for philosophy and for Western civilization.

25. In his first major work, *Being and Time* (1927), Heidegger still sought true knowledge in a priori structures found in the human mind. But later, after his "turning about," he sought a direct approach to Being itself.

26. It is with respect to his earlier work that Heidegger is called an existentialist.

27. There he was concerned with *Sinn* (sense or meaning), the absence of which was the problem of human existence. Basic concepts: thrownness, headbreaking, beings-in-the-world, everydayness, chatter, beings-unto-death, and project.

28. The cultural and intellectual poverty of the twentieth century is the result of the assumption that man is the measure of all things; an assumption, entrenched in Western civilization since Plato, that was found in its fullest flower in Nietzsche.

29. The later Heidegger: We must endeavor to catch a glimpse of Being as it shows itself, and not impose our thought on it. What is required is a new kind of thinking, such as already occurs in the best poetry. Through this new kind of thinking we may rediscover Being itself.

30. Heidegger's writings show a deep concern with the habitable world and with language.

Boxes

- Dostoyevsky's Notes from the Underground
  (Words from the "underground man")

- "The Death of Ivan Ilyich"
  (Tolstoy's story)

- The Trial
  (Kafka's novel)

- Profile: Albert Camus

- Life Is Absurd
  (Explains the existential predicament)

- The Just
  (Camus's play)

- Is Sartre Only for Atheists?
  (No)

- Profile: Jean-Paul Sartre

- Sartre and Kant on Ethics
  (Two versions of a universal principle?)

- Sartre and Heidegger
  (Their philosophies are different, despite the similarities)

- You Are What You Do
  (Explains Sartre's doctrine)

- Phenomena
  (An explication of this vital concept)

- Is This Idealism?
  (That is, is Husserl's philosophy idealism?)

- Profile: Martin Heidegger

- Heidegger and the Nazis
  (*Heidegger's support of Hitler*)

- Lost Lives
  (*Examples of lives lost to the inertia of everydayness*)

- Poetry and Philosophy
  (*About Heidegger's emphasis on poetry, with some examples of his own work*)

- Heidegger and Lao Tzu
  (*Concerning Heidegger's interest in Lao Tzu*)

Readings

7.1   Jean-Paul Sartre, from *Existentialism and Humanism*

Sartre explains existentialism and its most important concepts, including anguish and abandonment.

7.2   Albert Camus, from *The Myth of Sisyphus*

Reflections on the absurdity of the world.

Philosophers' Principal Works

- Søren Kierkegaard (1813–1855)
  Either/Or (1843)
  Philosophical Fragments (1844)
  The Concluding Unscientific Postscript (1846)

- Friedrich Nietzsche (1849–1900)
  The Birth of Tragedy (1872)
  Beyond Good and Evil (1886)
  Twilight of the Idols (1888)
  Ecce Home (1888)
  Thus Spoke Zarathustra (1883–1891)

- Arthur Schopenhauer (1788–1860)
  The World as Will and Idea (1818)
  The Basis of Morality (1841)
  "The Fourfold Root of the Principle of Sufficient Reason" (trans. 1888)

- Fyodor Dostoyevsky (1821–1881)
  Notes from the Underground (1864)
  Crime and Punishment (1866)
  The Idiot (1869)
  The Possessed (1871–1872)
  The Brothers Karamazov (1879–1880)

- Leo Tolstoy (1828–1910)
  War and Peace (1862–1869)
  Anna Karenina (1873–1876)
  "The Death of Ivan Ilyich" (1884)
  The Kreutzer Sonata (1889)

- Franz Kafka (1883–1924)
  Metamorphosis (1915)
  The Trial (1925)
  The Castle (1926)
  Amerika (1927)
  "The Judgment" (1945)

- Eugène Ionesco (1912–1994)
  The Bald Soprano (1950)
  Rhinoceros (1959)
  Present Past, Past Present (1968)
  Le Solitaire (1973)
  The Hermit (1974)

- Samuel Beckett (1906–1989)
  Murphy (1938)
  Molloy (1951)
  Malone Dies (1951)
  Waiting for Godot (1952)
  Endgame (1957)
  The Lost Ones (1972)

- Albert Camus (1913–1960)
  The Stranger (1946)
  The Plague (1948)
  The Rebel (1954)
  The Myth of Sisyphus (1955)
  Resistance, Rebellion and Death (1961)
  The First Man (1995)

- Jean-Paul Sartre (1905–1980)
    The Psychology of Imagination (1940)
    Being and Nothingness (1943)
    Existentialism and Humanism (1946)
    No Exit (1947)
    Nausea (1949)

- Edmund Husserl (1859–1938)
    Logical Investigations (1900)
    Ideas: General Introduction to Pure Phenomenology (1931)
    "Philosophy as a Rigorous Science" (published *in Phenomenology and the Crisis of Philosophy*, 1965)
    Cartesian Meditations (1960)

- Martin Heidegger (1889–1976)
    Being and Time (1927)
    What Is Metaphysics? (1929)
    Letter On Humanism (1949)
    Introduction to Metaphysics (1953)
    The End of Philosophy (1956)

Lecture-Discussion Ideas Related to Selected Questions

Two ideas on teaching Continental philosophy

Here are two things you might emphasize in a lecture on Continental philosophy.

The history of philosophy is sometimes spruced up a bit for beginning students by presenting it as a series of revolutions: Descartes's rejection of scholasticism; Kant's Copernican revolution and search for an epistemology that would not fall prey either to the speculative excesses of dogmatic metaphysicians nor to the sand traps in Hume's skepticism.

But not all philosophical developments are revolutionary. The Continental Rationalists continued the work of Descartes; Berkeley and Hume took up where Locke left off; the idealists subjected Kantian themes to further development. Philosophy evolves through continuation and refinement of past philosophies as well as through rejection of them.

And some philosophical developments are just simply innovations that don't seem to have terribly much to do with what has gone before, though instances of these are somewhat rarer. Zeno's proofs and Russell's theory of descriptions are examples of innovations. Hobbes's contractarianism might be cited as another example.

Continuation, revolution, and innovation—these are the three mechanisms by which philosophy generates its complex and unique history. Continental philosophy gives an example of each process, and this is one thing that might be emphasized in a discussion of it, as follows.

Schopenhauer, Kierkegaard, and Nietzsche were the revolutionaries. They were the strident critics of the pompous optimism of the Hegelian idealism. They laughed at Reason as the supposed governing principle and ineluctable destiny of the world. In rejecting idealism they broke new ground.

The existentialists continued the battle against idealism. But they weren't the first to jump the barricades. So they aren't really first-generation revolutionaries. The crunching break with tradition was made by their predecessors, and the existentialists tried to salvage something from the wreckage. That the world is irrational, that there is no cosmic plan for the universe and no march toward fulfillment of that plan—for the existentialists this was not a position that needed defending. It was the brutal, undeniable given. It required no argument, though it deserved vivid illustration. That the world is absurd is clear, they said. Now how are we supposed to live, given this, they asked.

Phenomenology, by contrast, can be viewed as a philosophical innovation. Yes, Husserl was aware of a crisis within Western civilization. But he found the cause of this crisis to be too little rationality rather than too much. And yes, he was influenced by his predecessors. But the influence of Brentano and Descartes and Kant and Hume—and mathematics—is more marked than is that of the Hegelians. His new approach, the phenomenological method, was essentially a philosophical invention.

Critical theory, as exemplified by Habermas (see chapter 13), is a continuation of the Marxist tradition, though it is more Marxian than Marxist. The deconstruction of Derrida broke with French structuralism; though billed as something "new," it seems to have odd affinities with the pragmatic tradition of Rorty (as opening up new possibilities of meaning). Foucault in his genealogy hearkened back to Nietzsche.

So, to repeat, you find the three mechanisms of philosophical evolution nicely represented in Continental philosophy.

Another aspect of Continental philosophy that ought to be put under the light is its emphasis on the human condition. In contrast with Eastern philosophy, philosophy in the West has tended to concern itself with otherworldly things (though there are some glaringly obvious exceptions to this—the Stoics, Spinoza, political philosophers). German idealism seems to leave the individual all too often the unknowing puppet of cunning absolute reason realizing itself in history, and existentialism's forerunners can be perceived as reacting to this aspect of idealism. Kierkegaard especially stressed the importance of the subject and the subject's anguished existence in the world. Likewise, the existentialists recognized the otherworldliness of Western philosophy and its apparent irrelevancy to the human condition and to the truly pressing problems of existence: injustice, alienation, banality, rootlessness, isolation, and lack of communication. Sartre saw the world as without any necessity and emphasized that the individual himself determines his own essential nature through his actions. Camus too, of course, sought to return thinking to an understanding of the human situation.

Of course, it is precisely because existentialism speaks to the individual that it tends to be so very much more popular with undergraduates than analysis, which is apt to be perceived as totally irrelevant to anything of importance.

15.   *Is most human conversation really "chatter"? Is most of your conversation really chatter?*

People seem to engage in small talk mainly for three reasons: (1) to avoid talking about embarrassing and unpleasant subjects—death, disease, pay cuts, and the like; (2) to dispel nervousness and anxiety: you find a lot of small talk on first dates; and (3) to procrastinate. Engaging in small talk for any of these reasons is perfectly normal and entirely healthy, up to a point.

But then some people engage in small talk more than is normal, and some people less. Extremes in either direction can be the reflection of psychological problems.

Chatter, however, isn't exactly the same as small talk. Or rather, it's small talk that is particularly trivial and tedious. But, to answer the question, human conversation is not mostly chatter. Whenever people really are trying to get something done—and that's pretty often, even for people on the 35-hour work week—and communicating with one another is essential to the task at hand, people don't generally chatter. They also don't usually chatter when they are seeking information or assistance (or giving them), though in some cases chatter can be the symptom of a deeper-level need. We don't permit students to waste our time with chatter, and neither do you.

Of course, much human conversation is about subjects that don't have much lasting significance. Yesterday's football game, for instance, is pretty trivial when measured on some finer scale; yet you do hear people going on about it, even those who are not even remotely affected by its outcome. We confess to being particularly annoyed by discussions of the comings and goings and doings of motion picture stars and other celebrities.

All in all, we are inclined to think that watching movies on the VCR has supplanted chatter as the most popular form of problem avoidance.

CHAPTER 8

The Pragmatic and Analytic Traditions

Main Points

1. On the continent of Europe, the assault on idealism began with the nihilistic attacks of Schopenhauer, Nietzsche, and the religious anti-idealism of Kierkegaard, reaching its summit with the development of existentialism. The philosophical focus in Britain and the United States in the twentieth century has been quite different.

2. <u>Pragmatism</u>

   Twentieth-century philosophy in the United States was shaped by pragmatism (or American pragmatism).

3. Pragmatists rejected the idea that there is fixed, absolute truth; instead, it is relative to a time and place and purpose and is thus ever-changing in light of new data.

4. C. S. Peirce: "The opinion which is fated to be ultimately agreed to by all who investigate, is what we mean by the truth." Truth has a communitarian aspect.

5. Peirce: Pragmatism is a rule for ascertaining the meaning of ideas. The meaning of a concept is the sum total of its practical consequences. For Peirce, that meant that most metaphysical concepts were meaningless or absurd.

6. William James: To determine either the meaning or the truth of an idea, one must evaluate its usefulness or workability—its "cash value." This is a more individualistic understanding of truth than Peirce's, though James would count as what works for the individual the findings of the community of scientific investigators.

7. James was also famous for the related theory that in some cases it is justifiable to choose or will to hold a belief because of the "vital good" it provides to a person, even if the evidence for and against the belief weighs in equally. If "the hypothesis of God" "works satisfactorily in the widest sense of the word," James said it was "true." (More on James in part 3 on the philosophy of religion.)

8. **John Dewey's** instrumentalism regarded thinking as problem solving rather than truth seeking. Dewey rejected both traditional realism ("the spectator theory of knowledge") and idealism, and regarded abstract speculation about so-called eternal truths as escapism.

9. As a social activist, Dewey had a significant effect on American educational, judicial, and legislative institutions.

10. Though pragmatism has been making a modest comeback in American philosophy departments, it was analytic philosophy, first developed in Britain, that became dominant in the United States.

11. Analytic Philosophy

    What analysis is. Analysis resolves complex propositions or concepts into simpler ones.

12. The evolution of analytic philosophy. **Bertrand Russell**, looking for a satisfactory account of numbers and mathematics, abandoned Absolute Idealism and adopted logicism, the thesis that the concepts of mathematics can be defined in terms of concepts of logic, and that all mathematical truths can be proved from principles of formal logic. (Gottlob Frege had undertaken to establish logicism independently of Russell.)

13. Russell's logicism involved the analysis of mathematical propositions; under the influence of colleague G. E. Moore, Russell began to think of the analytic method as promising to deliver the same indisputable results in other areas of philosophy as it did in the philosophy of mathematics.

14. **G. E. Moore** analyzed some commonsense beliefs about physical objects as well as certain propositions in moral philosophy.

15. **Gilbert Ryle**: The principal business of philosophy is to use analysis to dissolve traditional philosophical problems.

16. **Ludwig Wittgenstein**: The goal of analysis is to reduce complex descriptive propositions to their ultimately simple constituent propositions, which consist of "names" in combination, which would represent the ultimate simple constituents of reality.

17. The **logical positivists** (such as Moritz Schlick): Philosophy is not a theory but an activity the objective of which is the logical clarification of thought.

18. They proposed a verifiability criterion of meaning, according to which genuine propositions are either tautologies or are empirically verifiable.

19. The positivists regarded the pronouncements of metaphysics and theology as meaningless, and held value judgments to be expressions of emotion.

20. The positivists: Philosophy has as its only useful function the analysis of everyday and scientific language; it has no legitimate concern with the world apart from language.

21. Few analytic philosophers today subscribe to the verifiability criterion of meaning or accept the basic views of the logical positivists.

22. Many so-called analytic philosophers today do not regard analysis as the "proper" method of philosophy or think of analysis as one of their principal tasks. Wittgenstein came to repudiate analysis as the proper method of philosophy.

23. It is now widely held that many philosophically interesting claims and expressions cannot intelligibly be regarded as complexes subject to linguistic reduction.

24. **W. V. O. Quine**: It is questionable whether it is ever possible to say in some absolute sense what the meaning of an expression is.

25. In its broadest sense, a call for "analysis" today is simply a call for clarification.

26. Experience, language, and the world. Analytic epistemology and metaphysics has broadly focused on the interrelationship of experience, language, and the world; and the nature of mind.

27. Russell's logical atomism regarded the world not as an all-encompassing Oneness (as the Hegelians said it was), but as a collection of atomic facts, each logically independent of every other fact and not themselves composed of simpler or more basic facts.

28. Atomists: Because all complex propositions must in principle be resolvable into simpler propositions by analysis, there must be fundamental and absolutely simple propositions that cannot be resolved further and that are logically independent of each other. Corresponding to these "atomic" propositions are the fundamental or atomic facts.

29. Russell changed his mind over his lifetime as to the minimum that must be supposed to exist but generally he believed that this did not include many of things that "common sense" is inclined to say exist, such as physical objects and atoms and subatomic particles. What we think and say about these can be expressed in propositions that refer only to awareness or sense-data.

30. Russell: What we truly know is sense-data and what we believe exists, such as physical objects and such scientific entities as atoms and electrons, must be definable in terms of sense-data if those beliefs are to be philosophically secure.

31. Phenomenalism: The notion that propositions about physical and scientific objects are in theory expressible in propositions that refer only to sense-data.

32. Phenomenalism as a rebuttal to skepticism: the theory that propositions that refer to physical objects can be expressed in propositions that make reference only to sense-data.

33. Whether phenomenalism is sound rests on whether our supposed knowledge of an external world can be understood in purely sensory terms, whether "reality" reduces to "appearances."

34. Why phenomenalism was considered unsound: (1) there is no set of sense-data the having of which logically entails that you are experiencing a given physical object; (2) it is unclear that physical-object propositions that mention specific times and places could have equivalent sense-data propositions; (3) private language is impossible.

35. Philosophers are now questioning whether or not knowledge requires foundations at all.

36. Naturalized epistemology rests on psychology or the processes actually involved in the acquisition and revision of beliefs.

37. Antirepresentationalism. Quine's naturalized epistemology has become a leading alternative to foundationalism; in metaphysics Quine proposed a nonreductionistic alternative to phenomenalism; physical objects are theoretical posits, entities whose existence we in effect hypothesize in order to explain our sensory experience.

38. The Quinean view of objects as theoretical posits is consistent with realism (the thesis that reality consists of physical objects independent of the perceiving and knowing mind) but is also consistent with skepticism (because theoretical posits may not in fact exist).

39. Phenomenalism refutes skepticism only by denying realism (denying that objects are independent of our sense-data).

40. Underlying realism is the notion that true beliefs represent or correspond to reality; according to representationalism, a belief counts as knowledge only if it is a true belief, and a belief if true only if it is an accurate representation of the state of affairs that it is about.

41. The antirepresentationalism of **Richard Rorty** and others denies that mind or language contain or are representations of reality.

42. When we describe a belief as true we are simply praising that belief as having been proven relative to *our* standards of rationality.

43. Rorty's antirepresentationalism was anticipated by the pragmatists, especially Dewey. Pragmatic thought has entered analytical philosophy through philosophers such as Quine, Hilary Putnam, and Rorty.

44. The Philosophy of Mind

   Philosophy of mind seeks to understand (analyze) everyday psychological language and to encompass the research of psychologists, neuroscientists, computer scientists, linguists, artificial intelligence researchers, and other specialists.

45. Dualism. A human being has (or is) both a physical body and a nonphysical mind, and these two things are interactive. (Not all dualists believe the immaterial mind and the material body interact, but most dualists do, so dualism as used here, unless otherwise noted, refers to interactionist dualism.)

46. Difficulties in the theory: (1) characterization problem; (2) individuation problem; (3) emergence problem; (4) dependency problem; (5) no-necessity problem; (6) interaction problem; (7) understanding problem.

47. Many analytic philosophers reject dualism and tend to subscribe to the physicalist theories behaviorism, identity theory, or functionalism.

48. Behaviorism. As a methodological principle of **psychology**, behaviorism holds that fruitful psychological investigation confines itself to such psychological phenomena as can be behaviorally defined.

49. **Ryle**: **Philosophical** behaviorism is the doctrine that (1) There is no such thing as a nonphysical mind—there is "no ghost within the machine"; (2) Mental-state thing-words do not really denote things; statements in which such words appear are loose references to behaviors and behavioral dispositions; (3) Statements about a person's mental states cannot, despite (2), actually be translated into some set of statements about the person's behavior and behavioral dispositions.

50. Behaviorism seems to solve the interaction and no-necessity problems.

51. Identity theory. So-called mental phenomena are physical phenomena within the brain and central nervous system (CNS).

52. Among the adherents: Australian philosopher **J. J. C. Smart**.

53. Identity theory is easily confused with behaviorism, but it is a distinct theory. The identity theory holds that mind-states are brain states, that reference to a person's beliefs or thoughts is in fact reference to events and processes within that person's brain and nervous system. Philosophical behaviorism holds that the psychological vocabulary used in describing a person is just a shorthand way to talk about that person's behavioral dispositions.

54. Functionalism. Many physicalists question the identity theory (wherein each distinct mental state or process equates with one and only one brain state or process) since it is possible that a certain psychological state could be correctly ascribed to quite different physiological systems. It seems better to define a mental state by its function.

55. Functionalism explains why psychology is not reducible to neurology, but doesn't commit its adherents to questionable dualistic metaphysical notions.

56. If functionalism is correct, then while everything that happens may be physical, "straightforward reductivist physicalism" (*reducing* everything to physics) is unlikely.

Boxes

- Profile: John Dewey

- The Paradox of Analysis
  (*"Analyses are either incorrect or trivial"*)

- Profile: Bertrand Russell

- The World's Shortest Refutation of Skepticism
  (*"This, after all, you know, really is a finger. . ."*)

- Profile: Ludwig Wittgenstein

- The End of the Parade
  (*A shift in recent philosophy from the focus on the philosophies of specific individuals to an emphasis on philosophical ideas, such as foundationalism or representationalism*)

- Wittgenstein's Turnaround
  (*The main themes of Wittgenstein's* Tractatus *as compared with those of his* Philosophical Investigations)

- Awareness Without a Subject?
  (*Brief discussion of Russell's idea that only the awareness and not the subject that has the awareness is present in experience*)

- Sense-Data Not Mental?
  (No, at least as sense-data are viewed by Russell, Ayer, and others)

- Nonsense
  (A brief mention of Wittgenstein's problem in using language to represent how language represents the world)

- Private Languages?
  (The argument against their possibility)

- Nonpropositional Foundations
  (Could something other than a proposition quality as a foundation of knowledge?)

- The Big Issues
  (Why the work of analytic philosophers strikes outsiders as narrow and tedious)

- Abstract and Meaningless Philosophy?
  (Why philosophy of mind is not meaninglessly abstract)

- Popular Reasons for Believing That We Are Not Mere Matter
  (Eight reasons are given)

- Reasons for Doubting That the Mind Is Nonphysical
  (Seven reasons are given)

- Behaviorism, Pro and Con
  (Four difficulties)

- Ockham's Razor
  (If you don't have a reason to believe in something, don't)

- Current Issues in Physicalist Philosophies of Mind
  (Final authority problem; intentionality and propositional attitudes; subjectivity/privacy)

- Brentano and Intentionality
  (What it means to say that conscious states are "intentional")

- Profile: Luisa Maria Oliva Sabuco de Nantes Barerra

Readings

8.1   Elizabeth Anscombe, from *Metaphysics and the Philosophy of Mind*

How a leading analytic philosopher became hooked on philosophy.

8.2   J. J. C. Smart, from "Sensations and Brain Processes"

Smart explains identity theory, first by clarifying the nature of the equation between sensations and brain processes, and second by replying to objections to the view that sensation statements report processes in the brain.

8.3   Richard Rorty, from *Objectivity, Relativism, and Truth*

Rorty maintains that both realism *and* idealism have representationalist presuppositions in common, and that both views ought to be rejected by the antirepresentationalist.

Philosophers' Principal Works

- John Dewey (1859–1952)
  Reconstruction in Philosophy (1920)
  Human Nature and Conduct (1922)
  Experience and Nature (1925)
  The Quest for Certainty (1929)
  Art as Experience (1934)
  Freedom and Culture (1939)
  Problems of Men (1946)

- C. S. Peirce (1839–1914)
  "The Fixation of Belief" (1877)
  "How to Make Our Ideas Clear" (1878)
  "Man's Glassy Essence" (1892)
  "Pragmatism" (1905)

- William James (1842–1910)
  Principles of Psychology (1890)
  The Will to Believe and Other Essays in Popular Philosophy (1897)
  The Varieties of Religious Experience (1902)
  Pragmatism (1907)
  A Pluralistic Universe (1909)
  The Meaning of Truth (1909)
  Some Problems in Philosophy (1911)
  Essays in Radical Empiricism (1912)

- Bertrand Russell (1872–1970)
  - *The Principles of Mathematics* (1903)
  - "On Denoting" (1905)
  - "On the Relations of Universals and Particulars" (1911)
  - *Principia Mathematica* (1910–1913)
  - *Our Knowledge of the External World* (1914)
  - *Mysticism and Logic* (1918)
  - "The Philosophy of Logical Atomism" (1918)
  - *The Analysis of Mind* (1921)
  - *The Analysis of Matter* (1927)
  - *Marriage and Morals* (1929)
  - *An Inquiry Into Meaning and Truth* (1940)
  - *Human Knowledge, Its Scope and Limits* (1948)
  - *Why I Am Not a Christian* (1957)
  - *My Philosophical Development* (1959)

- Gottlob Frege (1848–1925)
  - *Begriffsschrift* (1879)
  - *Grundlagen der Arithmetik* (1884)
  - "Function and Concept" (1891)
  - "Concept and Object" (1892)
  - "Sense and Reference" (1892)

- G. E. Moore (1873–1958)
  - *Principia Ethica* (1903)
  - *Philosophical Studies* (1922)
  - *Philosophical Papers* (1959)

- Ludwig Wittgenstein (1889–1951)
  - *Notebooks* (1914–1916)
  - *Tractatus Logico-philosophicus* (1922)
  - *Philosophical Investigations* (1953)
  - *Remarks on the Foundations of Mathematics* (1956)
  - *The Blue and Brown Books* (1958)
  - *Philosophische Bemerkungen* (1964)

- Moritz Schlick (1882–1936)
  - *Allgemeine Erkenntnislehre* (1918)
  - *The Problems of Ethics* (1930)

- A. J. Ayer (1910–1989)
  - *Language, Truth and Logic* (1936)
  - *The Foundations of Empirical Knowledge* (1940)
  - *Thinking and Meaning* (1947)
  - *The Problem of Knowledge* (1956)
  - *The Concept of a Person* (1963)

- Gilbert Ryle (1900–1976)
  "Systematically Misleading Expressions" (1931)
  Philosophical Argument (1945)
  The Concept of Mind (1949)
  Dilemmas (1954)

- W. V. O. Quine (1908–)
  From a Logical Point of View (1953)
  Methods of Logic (1959)
  Word and Object (1960)
  The Web of Belief (1970)
  Theories and Things (1981)
  Quiddities (1987)

- Hilary Putnam (1926–)
  Representation and Reality (1988)
  Realism with a Human Face (1990)
  Renewing Philosophy (1992)

- Richard Rorty (1931–)
  Philosophy and the Mirror of Nature (1979)
  Consequences of Pragmatism (1982)
  Contingency, Irony, and Solidarity (1989)
  Objectivity, Relativism, and Truth (1991)
  Essays on Heidegger and Others (1991)
  Truth and Progress (1998)
  Achieving Our Country (1998)

- J. J. C. Smart (1920–)
  Philosophy and Scientific Realism (1963)

- Franz Brentano (1838–1917)
  From the Manifold Meaning of Being in Aristotle (1862)
  Psychology from an Empirical Standpoint (1874)
  Original Moral Knowledge (1889)
  Truth and Evidence (1930)

- Luisa Maria Oliva Sabuco de Nantes Barerra (1562– ?)
  New Philosophy of Human Nature (1587)

Lecture-Discussion Ideas Related to Selected Questions

2.   *What is accomplished by the use of philosophical analysis?*

For one thing, analysis can help us evaluate, say, two competing metaphysical systems. There are no hard rules that we can apply in a mechanical fashion for choosing between alternative metaphysical theories. Among the factors many analytical philosophers say should be considered are these:

a.   Clarity is important. Some metaphysical theories are pretty vague on important details, and that's a weakness. Take Hobbes's materialist metaphysics. Hobbes's account of sensation is really pretty murky, no? According to Hobbes we experience the world as consisting of objects with certain properties. But what's really out there, matter in motion, doesn't really possess those properties we sense, or at least not all of them. Hobbes's account of how matter is sensed as a group of objects that have properties that matter itself supposedly does not have is sketchy at best. Or take Cartesian dualism: Descartes leaves us with hardly even a vague idea how mind-body interaction takes place.

b.   Consistency is a must. If your theory is that mind and body interact but the details of your theory make it impossible that they could interact, your theory is in trouble. Descartes's dualism has been charged with precisely this inconsistency.

c.   It is an important shortcoming in a theory if it forces us to make unnecessary assumptions or is unnecessarily complicated or requires us to posit unnecessary entities. Aristotle thought that Plato's Theory of Forms did all these things.

(Of course, proponents and opponents of a theory will invariably disagree as to what really is an unnecessary assumption or posit and what really is unnecessarily complicated.)

d.   Are there any empirical tests that would tend to confirm or disconfirm the theory? Many analytic philosophers would regard it as a pretty serious weakness in a metaphysical theory if there were no conceivable tests for its correctness. For example, suppose someone proposes that everything is an illusion. How could you test this theory?

Granted, some of the logical positivists had it as analytic that *no* metaphysical theories are testable. But you have to wonder. Hobbes's materialism, for example, certainly qualifies as a metaphysical theory if anything does, and it generates testable hypotheses. For example, if Hobbes's materialism is true, then you would expect that signs of mental life would cease if the person's brain stopped functioning.

e.   Of course, a theory should not generate predictions that turn out to be false. Epiphenomenalism, the theory that brain states can affect mind states but the reverse does not hold, would lead one to predict that psychosomatic illness would not occur. Yes, epiphenomenalists do have explanations for psychosomatic illness that make the latter jibe with the epiphenomenalism, but the fact that they find it necessary to proffer these explanations shows right there that there are difficulties.

f.   The more ad hoc patch-ups a theory requires, the weaker it is. The theory of reincarnation, for instance, requires its proponents to reconcile the idea that we have all lived before with the fact that more humans are alive now than in the past. The proponents also must reconcile the idea that we acquire some or all of our essential traits and characteristics from past lives with what we know about genetics and developmental psychology. That epiphenomenalism has to be patched up to account for apparently psychosomatic illnesses we've already mentioned.

g.   Everything else being equal, if one theory violates principles of common sense in certain respects and the other doesn't, that would be some reason for favoring the latter. It's not that common sense must be right, but it probably represents at least some collective wisdom. The burden of proof is on anyone who proposes a theory that runs counter to common sense to show why we should accept it.

Again, you cannot just sit down with one theory on the right and another on the left and check off their virtues as you would two automobiles. But being aware of some of the factors that serve to weaken a theory is at least a first step toward finding a theory worth believing in.

A note on what might be called "the paradox of definition."

The paradox of *analysis* is explained as clearly as we can explain it in the box by that title in the text. Expressed loosely, the paradox is that an analysis is either incorrect or trivial.

A similar paradox, one that students find less complicated, might be entitled "the paradox of definition." Here's how it goes:

Consider a definition of a trombone as a brass wind instrument whose pitch is adjusted by a slide. If this definition—"A trombone is a brass wind instrument whose pitch is adjusted by a slide"—is correct, then it means the same as "A trombone is a trombone." That is, if the definition is correct, then it is trivial. And if it is not trivial, it is incorrect. The same problem supposedly attends all definitions.

A similar difficulty pertains to statements that equate names, and might be called "the paradox of identical names":

Take the statement "Mark Twain was Samuel Clemens." Since the statement is true, it must mean the same as "Mark Twain was Mark Twain." But, obviously, anyone who states that Mark Twain was Samuel Clemens presumably does not think he is stating merely that Mark Twain was Mark Twain.

Frege resolved the last problem, that concerning the identity of two different names, by distinguishing between the reference of a name—that's the person or thing that the name refers to or denotes, in this case the individual who wrote *Tom Sawyer*—and the "sense" of the name. "Mark Twain" and "Samuel Clemens" thus *refer* to the same thing, but have a different *sense*.

A similar distinction, one introduced by J. S. Mill, is sometimes used to resolve the paradox of definition. A term such as "trombone" has both a *denotation*—that's the objects to which the term is properly applied—and a *connotation*—that's the characteristics that anything to which the term properly applies must have. Then the definition "A trombone is a brass wind instrument whose pitch is adjusted by a slide" just gives the connotation of the word "trombone": it does not set forth a synonym for it.

Neither of these responses quite works for resolving the paradox of analysis, for here the two things "X" and "Y" that are said to mean the same are not names or terms but entire propositions, and a proposition doesn't really have a denotation, reference, sense, or connotation. Nevertheless, the solutions to the paradox of definition and the paradox of identical names do show that one expression "X" and another expression "Y" can be said to "mean the same" or be "equivalent" even though "Y" cannot be substituted for "X" (or vice versa) in all contexts. But then, that was already clear to common sense, if not to philosophy: Let "X" be "He is dead" and let "Y" be *Er ist tod.* Here "X" and "Y" mean the same, but are not substitutable one for the other in every context.

All in all, we almost think it is more difficult to explain the paradox of analysis than to explain ways of resolving it.

7.   *"If X might exist but we have no reason to suppose that it actually does exist, then as metaphysicians we should not concern ourselves with X." Why is this true? Why not?*

The trouble with this excellent principle that we philosophers all love and cherish is that it can often leave the important work undone. For the important question often is, When is a consideration a legitimate reason? In real cases people will just simply disagree as to whether there are legitimate reasons for supposing that whatever it is exists. Those who believe in ghosts, for example, are apt to think there are good reasons for believing in ghosts, and will not think the principle threatens the truth of their belief.

Similar remarks can be made about more traditional statements of Ockham's razor, for example, "Entities are not to be multiplied without necessity" (which formulation Ockham himself apparently did not use) and "What is done with fewer assumptions is done in vain with more." Just when are postulated entities unnecessary and assumptions vainly made? Situations do arise in which it is agreed on all hands that an explanation or theory posits entities needlessly or makes unnecessary assumptions, but people who disagree as to whether God or ghosts or space aliens (etc.) are real are also apt to disagree over the *necessity* of postulating them and of making the associated assumptions.

Consider the theist who says that God exists because the universe cannot have caused itself. An agnostic may reply that the theist postulates unnecessary entities, for whether or not we bring God into the picture there is something—either the universe or God—that caused itself. The theist, of course, is likely to think that there are reasons for supposing that the universe cannot cause itself that do not apply to an immateriality.

Incidentally, sometimes students seem to fail to distinguish between the principle "If there is no reason to suppose that something exists then don't say that the thing does" and the principle "If there is no reason to suppose that something exists then the thing doesn't."

Whenever we employ Ockham's razor we try to make it clear that our principle is not the second one, because otherwise someone always assumes that it is.

14.   *Present some reasons for believing that a human being is not a purely physical thing.*

The box entitled "Popular Reasons for Believing That We Are Not Mere Matter" contains several reasons. Here we will sketch physicalist rejoinders to these assorted arguments, for discussion.

a.   People, unlike physical objects, have feelings, emotion, thoughts, and beliefs and can perform lots of acts purely physical things cannot. The best explanation of these facts is that people have something that purely physical things don't have, something nonphysical.

—   *Rejoinder*: Yes, the best explanation of these facts is indeed that people have something that nonthinking things don't have, but that something doesn't have to be nonphysical. It could just be the vastly complex human brain and nervous system.

b.   People, unlike physical objects, have free will, which they wouldn't have if their minds were mere physical things.

—   *Rejoinder*: First, it isn't clear that humans do have free will. Second, it isn't clear that physical things could not have free will, if by having free will is meant merely that one could have acted differently in the same circumstances. Third, it isn't clear how, if humans viewed as purely physical could not have free will, having a nonphysical mind could remedy that deficiency.

c.   People are creative and have aesthetic sensibility—impossibilities for mere blind material things.

—   *Rejoinder*: We really don't know what creative ability or aesthetic sensibility are. A chess-playing computer would seem to act creatively to a human opponent who did not understand how the computer was programmed, and it may be that so-called creative human actions are the result of the "programming" done on humans by experience. Or, human creativity could just be the result of electrical disturbances in the human brain, misfirings of neurons, or whatnot. As for aesthetic sensibility—again, what is it? Humans are moved by poetry and music (some are, anyway), but they are also moved by pleasures of the palate and bedroom. What, then, is pleasure other than an internal stimulus to repeat or renew or continue an activity, a phenomenon that can be given a physiological explanation, one that would not require mention of anything nonphysical?

d.   People can sometimes override the constraints of physics, as when they overcome a terminal disease through exertion of will. People often demonstrate the power of mind over matter.

—   *Rejoinder*: There really is absolutely no evidence whatsoever that people can override the constraints of physics. If ten percent of those with some disease survive, you can be sure that the ninety percent who do not survive exert their "will" just as strenuously as those who do survive. The only demonstrated power that mind has over matter is that which is evident in ordinary volition, as when you move your arm, and it is not clear in ordinary volition that the mind that moves the arm is anything other than the brain.

e.   People can have knowledge of nonmaterial things, like the truths of mathematics. Therefore they are not themselves totally physical.

—   *Rejoinder*: For some reason this argument seems to be very popular with students who wish to defend dualism. Unfortunately, it is difficult to understand, and the conclusion seems to be a non sequitur. Is the idea that, because we can have knowledge of the truths of mathematics, we must share some of the immateriality of those truths? Would a fair parallel be arguing that, since we can have knowledge of horses, we must be partially equine? Also, mathematical truths have other features than immateriality; for example, they are eternal. Would it be acceptable to argue that, since we have knowledge of these truths, we must be eternal? Why is it the immateriality feature of mathematical truths that we must share rather than some other feature?

Concerning another matter, handheld calculators can give the correct answer to arithmetical questions. Presumably, however, the dualist who proposes the argument stated above will deny that handheld calculators have knowledge. The dualist must therefore be cautious not to beg the question by assuming as an unstated premise that only nonmaterial things can have knowledge.

f.   It is possible to doubt the existence of any given physical thing, but it is not possible to doubt the existence of your own mind. Therefore your mind is not a physical thing.

—   *Rejoinder*: The underlying principle here seems to be this: if it is possible to doubt the existence of X but not possible to doubt the existence of Y, then X is not Y. This principle is doubtful. Imagine Samuel Clemens being struck a blow on the head and forgetting that he wrote books as Mark Twain. Mark Twain, he believes, is just a fictitious character like Uncle Sam. When someone tries to tell him that he, Samuel Clemens, is Mark Twain, he reasons: I can doubt the existence of Mark Twain but I cannot possibly doubt the existence of Samuel Clemens. Therefore I am not Mark Twain.

g.   Beliefs and thoughts have properties that physical things by definition cannot have. Beliefs, for instance, are true or false. Physical things are not. So beliefs and thoughts are not physical. Conversely, physical things have properties that beliefs and thoughts cannot have, properties like location, density, temperature, and so forth. The same conclusion follows.

—   *Rejoinder*: Following the contemporary philosopher John Searle, we must distinguish between the global features of a person and the microfeatures of the neurons and molecules that make up the person. The global features will then have certain properties that the neurons and molecules do not have. For example, a global feature of a person is that he or she has beliefs, things that are true or false. Although the neurons and molecules that make up the person do not have those properties, the person is still a physical thing. Computers can play chess but silicon chips and electronic circuitry can't; still, computers are nothing but silicon chips and electronic circuitry. Water molecules are triangular and in constant motion, and water is not. Yet water is nothing but H_2O molecules. And so on.

h.   I have knowledge of my mental states, but it is not gained through observation. Physical states, on the other hand, I find out about only through observation. So physical things and my mind states are essentially different.

—   *Rejoinder*: Essentially the argument begs the question, since if the physicalist is correct, it turns out that brain states are knowable through introspection and that therefore the second premise is false.

A note on the individuation problem.

The individuation problem is this:

Here is a fact: Bruder and Moore cannot have only one mind between the two of them.

If minds were physical, this fact would be easily explained, because Bruder and Moore occupy separate locations and a physical thing cannot occupy two separate locations at the same time. Those who believe that the mind is nonphysical, however, cannot explain this fact, because nonphysical things don't occupy space. (Sharper students may object that shapes occupy space, and are not physical things. Shapes, however, are not really things at all. They are universals.) Given this, those who believe that the mind is nonphysical cannot cite the fact that Moore and Bruder are in different places as their explanation for why Moore and Bruder must have different minds. So their theory does not explain as much as does physicalism, according to which minds do occupy space.

We don't know of a good rejoinder to this objection to the idea that the mind is nonphysical. Those who believe that the mind is nonphysical cannot believe that minds occupy space, since if minds did they would be physical. But if minds don't occupy space (according to those who believe that the mind is nonphysical), there isn't an explanation for why Bruder and Moore do not have the same mind. You could object that a boundary or a point is a nonphysical thing that, despite being nonphysical and not occupying space, cannot be in two separate places at the same time. But boundaries and points are abstractions, and minds, presumably, are not abstract things. Those who believe that the mind is nonphysical cannot argue that a mind is a point or a boundary.

The only alternative left for those who believe that the mind is nonphysical is to say that nonphysical things can occupy space. But if we permit nonphysical things to occupy space, there is no distinguishing them from physical things.

CHAPTER 9

Moral Philosophy

Main Points

1. Ethics or moral philosophy is the study of moral judgments, which are value judgments about what is virtuous and base, just and unjust, morally right and wrong, morally good and bad or evil, morally proper and improper, and so on.

2. Since many questions can be asked about moral judgments, ethics encompasses many issues. The most important question of ethics, however, is simply which moral judgments are correct?

3. The Early Greeks

   Sophists and **Socrates**: Moral judgments must be supported by reasons.

4. Socrates was also concerned with the meaning of words that signify moral virtues, such as justice, piety, and courage.

5. Socrates: Wrongness of behavior is due to ignorance.

6. Plato. Theory of Forms: At the apex of all Forms is the Form of the Good. Corollary: Since the Forms define true reality, individual things are real only insofar as they partake of the Form of the Good. Additional corollary: Evil is unreal.

7. Plato: Since Forms are apprehended by reason, one should strive for knowledge of the Good and hence be ruled by reason. One ruled by reason exhibits four cardinal virtues: temperance, courage, wisdom, and justice, and has a well-ordered soul: virtue is its own reward.

8. <u>A compete ethical theory.</u> Plato's theory is a complete ethical theory because it (1) identifies an ultimate source of all value, (2) sets forth a metaphysical justification for accepting this source as ultimate, (3) stipulates a fundamental moral principle, (4) provides a rationale for accepting the principle as universally binding, (5) specifies how knowledge of the supreme intrinsic good is obtained, and (6) holds that obedience to the moral principle is motivated.

9. <u>Aesara, the Lucanian.</u> The Greek philosopher **Aesara of Lucania** taught that *all* morally significant decisions, whether regarding families or the state, should reflect the appropriate proportions of reason, willpower, and such positive emotions as love. Her analysis of the soul was similar to Plato's: she said that the human psyche had three parts—the mind, spiritedness, and desire.

10. <u>Aristotle.</u> The first great ethical naturalist, Aristotle held that our highest good—our natural objective—is happiness, which consists in two things: enjoyment and the exercise and development of the capacity to reason.

11. Aristotle: Virtue is the exercise of our capacity to reason, and there are two kinds of virtues: intellectual and moral.

12. Aristotle: Virtue is a matter of habit; a person's pleasures reveal his moral character. Specific moral virtues (such as courage) are the mean between extremes.

13. Though both Plato and Aristotle were proponents of what is now called virtue ethics, for Plato the Good was a nonnatural Form; for Aristotle, the good (for humans) is what human beings actually seek (happiness, properly understood). For Plato, the moral good transcends nature; for Aristotle the moral good finds its grounding *in* human nature.

14. <u>Epicureanism and Stoicism</u>

   The four main schools of philosophy following Aristotle were the Epicureans, the Stoics, the Skeptics, and the Neoplatonists.

15. **Epicureanism** and **Stoicism** were naturalistic ethical theories.

16. <u>Epicureanism.</u> **Epicurus:** We ought to seek the pleasant life, which comes with satisfaction of desires that are natural and the satisfaction of which is necessary for a pleasant life. Natural desires that need not be satisfied may be satisfied if doing so does not lead to discomfort or pain. Unnatural/unnecessary desires ought never to be satisfied.

17. **The Stoics.** We ought to seek the untroubled life, which comes through neutral acceptance of the natural order of things.

18. All that occurs is in accordance with natural law (reason): Whatever happens is the inevitable outcome of the logic of the universe; all that happens has a reason; so whatever happens is for the best. We ought to remain uninvolved emotionally in our fate, and our lives will be untroubled. **Epictetus** was among the most famous of the Stoics.

19. Christianizing Ethics

    St. Augustine. Christianized Platonic ethics: God is the source of all that is real and good.

20. Augustine explained evil by adapting the Platonic view: Natural evil is the absence of reality; moral evil is disordered love—turning from God.

21. Augustine: Virtue and sin are conditions of the soul; what matters is not the person's good deeds but the state of mind (intent) in which the person acts.

22. St. Hildegard of Bingen. This medieval German Benedictine nun said mystical experience provides a form of knowledge unavailable to pure rational introspection.

23. Heloise and Abelard

    The ethics of the medieval French philosopher **Heloise** has two primary components—(a) true love for another, whether platonic or sexual, is completely unselfish and asks nothing and (b) the morality of the act resides in the intention of the actor. Her love affair with Abelard, her philosophy teacher, was governed, she felt, by these precepts (though it turned out that Abelard's love for Heloise seemed purely sexual).

24. **Abelard**: Sin does not consist in acting on evil desires, or even in having them, but in consenting to act on evil desires.

25. St. Thomas Aquinas. **Aquinas** adapted Aristotelian thought for Christianity. Goodness for humans is happiness.

26. Aquinas: Natural law is the law of reason, which leads us to our natural end insofar as we follow it. God's divine law, revealed to us through God's grace, guides us to happiness everlasting.

27. Aquinas: There are two sets of virtues, the natural virtues such as courage, temperance, justice, and prudence, and the higher virtues of faith, love, and hope.

28. Hobbes and Hume

    Hobbes. An ethical naturalist, **Hobbes** espoused a philosophy of relentless materialism. "Good" and "evil" denote only what one desires or detests; justice and injustice consist in the keeping or breaking of covenants.

29. Hobbes: People live in a state of war or peace. The natural state of mankind is war; peace is possible only under a social contract that transfers the collective power of a people to a sovereign power. Only under a sovereign power do genuine covenants, hence justice and injustice, exist.

30. Hobbes affirmed natural laws (for him, value-neutral principles discovered by reason for one's preservation) and the "natural right" to use all means to defend ourselves.

31. Hobbes was important for his descriptivism.

32. Hume. Moral principles, **Hume** argued, are neither divine edicts nor discoverable by reason.

33. Value judgments are based on emotion, not reason. Hume: Moral and all other value judgments are based on emotion; actions we find morally praiseworthy or blameworthy create within us feelings of pleasure or displeasure, respectively.

34. Benevolence. Judgments of moral approval are expressions of the pleasure that we experience when presented with behavior that reflects a benevolent character.

35. Goodness consists in traits and actions that promote the welfare of people (this idea was appropriated in the nineteenth century by the utilitarians).

36. Hume's inquiries set the stage for subsequent ethical philosophy.

37. Can there be ethics after Hume? Options for ethics after Hume are four: (1) Despite Hume, ethics might seek to establish that morality can be grounded on reason or on God—**Kant's** option. (2) It might try to find objective sources of moral standards other than reason or God—the utilitarians' option. (3) It might seek to determine how one should act given the absence of objective moral standards—the existentialists' option. (4) It might abandon the search for moral standards altogether and concentrate on ethical descriptivism—the option of analytic philosophy.

38. Kant

   Kant held that reason alone can ascertain principles of morality.

39. The supreme principle of morality. Kant: A moral rule is universal and absolute. Thus, the supreme prescription of morality is to act in such a way that you could, rationally, will the principle on which you act to be a universal law.

40. And a moral rule may be expressed as a categorical imperative.

41. <u>Why you should do what you should do.</u> You should do what you should do because it is right. The consequences of an act, according to Kant, do not determine whether the act is good; only the intent or "will" with which it is taken does that.

42. Rationality is the source of all value, so the rational will is alone inherently good.

43. Another formulation of the categorical imperative: Treat rational beings (e.g., humans) in every instance as ends and never just as means.

44. <u>The Utilitarians</u>

   A different view was taken by the utilitarians, **Jeremy Bentham** and **John Stuart Mill**: The rightness of an action is identical with the happiness it produces as a consequence, with everyone considered.

45. <u>Bentham.</u> Happiness is pleasure, and positive ethical value-words have meaning only when defined in terms of pleasure. Pleasure can be evaluated only with reference to quantitative criteria. Bentham is often called an act-utilitarian.

46. <u>Mill.</u> Some pleasures are better than others; quality as well as quantity of pleasure is a factor in moral value. Mill is often referred to as a rule-utilitarian.

47. <u>Friedrich Nietzsche</u>

   Nietzsche took the view that there were basically just two moralities: master morality (the morality of the noble individual) and slave morality (the morality of the masses, epitomized by Christian ethics). Moralities were matters of social institution; master morality invigorated the race whereas slave morality was a denial of life.

48. Nietzsche saw his this-worldly philosophy as a celebration of the will to power, which finds its highest expression in the noble individual who has risen beyond the slave categories of "good" and "evil."

Boxes

- Ethical Skepticism
   (Explains ethical skepticism, and relates the Sophists to it)

- Relativism
   (Contrasts descriptive with ethical relativism and indicates difficulties in both)

- Subjectivism
   (Brief explanation of subjectivism, with criticism)

- Plato and Divine-Command Ethics
  (Is something right because the gods commend it, or do they commend it because it is right?)

- Is the Objective World Value-Neutral?
  (That's the opinion of most, nowadays. Plato had a different view)

- Instrumental and Intrinsic Ends
  (The difference explained)

- The Good Life
  (The value of philosophy)

- The Go-for-It Philosophy of Aristippus
  (Also explains Cyrenaicism)

- Diogenes the Dog
  (Also mentions Antisthenes, and the Cynics)

- Profile: St. Hildegard of Bingen

- Profile: Heloise

- Egoism
  (Descriptive and prescriptive egoism both are covered)

- Is Altruism Really Egoism?
  (Explains a difficulty in the idea that it is)

- Character Again
  (Hume on character)

- Cold-Blooded Murder
  (The expression supports Hume's belief that moral judgments are not the offspring of reason)

- Me-First Heroes
  (How is it that me-first egoism became as popular as it is?)

- Kant, Reason, and Morals
  (Emphasizes Kant's principle that reason alone can determine whether or not an act is morally right)

- Breaking Promises
  (Explains that for Kant the maxim "Break your promises!" cannot be universalized; but that doesn't mean that, given his principles, you should never break a promise)

- Profile: Jeremy Bentham

- Hedonism
  (Explains psychological and ethical hedonism, Butler's refutation of the former, egoistic ethical hedonism, and universalistic ethical hedonism)

- The Paradox of Hedonism
  (What it is, according to Sidgwick)

Readings

9.1   Plato, from *Gorgias*

Socrates's answer to Callicles, who claims the best life is the life of following one's appetites or desires.

9.2   Epicurus, from "Epicurus to Menoeceus"

Epicurus's recommendations for the good life.

9.3   Epictetus, from "The Encheiridion"

Several pieces of sage Stoic advice, always popular with students.

9.4   Immanuel Kant, from *Foundations of the Metaphysics of Morals*

This is the passage in which Kant elucidates his famous Categorical Imperative.

9.5   John Stuart Mill, from *Utilitarianism*

Mill's exposition of the "greatest happiness principle" in terms of the quality of pleasures.

9.6   Friedrich Nietzsche, from *Beyond Good and Evil*

An effort by Nietzsche toward a "revaluation of values" as he contrasts master morality with slave morality.

Philosophers' Principal Works

- Socrates (c. 470–399 B.C.)

- Plato (c. 427–347 B.C.)
  Republic
  Theaetetus
  Symposium
  Parmenides
  Timaeus
  Apology
  Crito
  Phaedo

- Aesara of Lucania (c. 350 B.C.)
  Book on Human Nature

- Aristotle (384–322 B.C.)
  Physics
  Metaphysics
  On the Soul (De Anima)
  Nicomachean Ethics
  Politics
  The Organon of logical works

- Epicurus (341–270 B.C.)
  "To Herodotus"
  "To Pythocles"
  "To Menoeceus"
  "Cardinal Tenets"

- Aristippus (435–350 B.C.)

- Zeno (334–262 B.C.)

- Cleanthes (303–233 B.C.)
  "Hymn to Zeus"

- Cicero (106–43 B.C.)
  On Oratory
  On Duties
  On Fate
  De Re Publica
  De Legibus

- Seneca (c. 4 B.C. –A.D. 65)
  Moral Essays
  Moral Letters
  Ten Tragedies

- Marcus Aurelius (A.D. 121–180)
  Meditations

- Epictetus (60–117)
  Discourses

- Diogenes (fourth century B.C.)
  Republic

- Augustine (354–430)
  Confessions
  De Genesi ad Litteram
  De Trinitate
  The City of God

- Hildegard of Bingen (1098–1179)
  Scivias
  Liber Vitae Meritorum
  De Operatione Dei

- Heloise (1100/1101–1163)
  Epistolae Heloissae
  Problemata Heloissae

- Thomas Aquinas (1225–1274)
  On Being and Essence (1253)
  Truth (Quaestiones Disputatae de Veritate [1256–1259])
  Summa Contra Gentiles (1258–1260)
  On the Power of God (1265)
  Summa Theologica (1265–1269)
  In Librum de Causis (1271)

- Thomas Hobbes (1588–1679)
  De Cive (1642)
  De Corpore Politico (1650)
  Leviathan (1651)
  The Questions Concerning Liberty, Necessity, and Chance (1656)
  De Corpore (1665)
  Behemoth (1682)

- David Hume (1711–1776)
    A Treatise of Human Nature (1739–1740)
    An Enquiry Concerning Human Understanding (1748)
    An Enquiry Concerning the Principles of Morals (1751)
    Dialogues Concerning Natural Religion (1779)

- Immanuel Kant (1724–1804)
    Critique of Pure Reason (1781)
    Prolegomena to Any Future Metaphysics (1783)
    Foundations of the Metaphysics of Morals (1785)
    Critique of Practical Reason (1788)
    Critique of Judgment (1790)

- Jeremy Bentham (1748–1832)
    A Fragment of Government (1776)
    An Introduction to the Principles of Morals and Legislation (1789)
    The Book of Fallacies (1824)
    Deontology (1834)

- John Stuart Mill (1806–1873)
    A System of Logic (1843)
    On Liberty (1859)
    Utilitarianism (1863)
    The Subjection of Women (1869)
    Autobiography and Literary Essays (1873)

- Henry Sidgwick (1838–1900)
    The Methods of Ethics (first edition, 1874)
    Outlines of the History of Ethics (1886)

- Friedrich Nietzsche (1849–1900)
    The Birth of Tragedy (1872)
    Beyond Good and Evil (1886)
    Twilight of the Idols (1888)
    Ecce Home (1888)
    Thus Spoke Zarathustra (1883–1891)

Lecture-Discussion Ideas Related to Selected Questions

11. *Can you control your attitude if you cannot control your fate?*

The Stoic idea that you can't control what happens to you so you should accept what happens as for the best is attractive to beginning students. Maybe they should be aware of the difficulties in this idea. If you have no control over what happens to you, then you have no control of your body, since if you have control of your body, you can have at least some effect on what happens to you. If you jump into the ocean after having tied a crankshaft around your ankle you have a fairly good chance of drowning. So the fundamental problem facing anyone who thinks you cannot control what happens to you but can control your attitude is reconciling a belief in determinism of the body with the belief in free-will of the mind.

The two beliefs are not outright contradictories, we suppose. As long as you hold that what happens in the mind is independent of what happens to the body, then you could consistently retain both beliefs. But if what happens to the body affects your thoughts and attitudes, then the total determinism of the body will undermine the freedom of the mind; and if your thoughts and attitudes affect what the body does, then the freedom of the mind will undo the total determinism of the body.

Few beginning students, if any, are likely to subscribe to a complete independence of thought and behavior. But if you put the question to them just that way—"How many of you subscribe to a complete independence of thought and behavior?"—what they are most likely to do is fall asleep.

One strategy that might work is to begin by asking a simple question: "Can your thoughts and attitudes change without there being some sort of change within your brain?" The answer almost certainly will be "no." As a next step, point out that, if a change in thoughts requires that there be some sort of change in your brain, then, if you really can control your thoughts, when you do so you will affect what happens to your brain. This means that, if you can control your thoughts, what happens to your body is not completely determined, since your brain is a part of your body.

The strategy might awaken slumbering epiphenomenalists (though we doubt it) who will say that the thought-changes don't *cause* the brain-changes. Their argument will be that thought-changes may always be accompanied by (the very same) brain-changes but yet the latter are not caused by the thought-changes but by something in the physical world.

This argument cannot be refuted as a matter of bad logic. But you can ridicule it.

Another strategy would be to run things in reverse and ask whether anyone in the class doubts that there are psychotropic or mood-altering drugs. Assuming that no one disputes the power of certain drugs to affect one's moods, you might then ask the class to suppose that fate has so arranged things that a Stoic has been injected with such a drug.

So much for controlling your attitudes.

This strategy too might prompt clever students to indulge in some reverse-epiphenomenalistic (hypophenomenalism, isn't it called?) maneuvering. Someone might argue that it isn't the *drugs* that affect the person's mood: what has happened is that an attack of weak will in overcoming mood changes has just happened to coincide with the injection of the drug.

Rest assured that most students will not find this maneuver very plausible.

17.   *Do we always act selfishly? Explain.*

As every philosophy instructor knows, someone in every introductory philosophy class maintains that people always act selfishly, and usually he or she is able to out-argue anyone who has a different opinion.

"We always act selfishly," the person will say. "Even when you help someone else, you're just doing it because it brings you pleasure."

The traditional rebuttal is to point out that you wouldn't derive pleasure from helping someone else unless you had the desire to help him or her; that having the desire to help the other person is logically prior to getting pleasure from doing so.

The rejoinder to the rebuttal, inevitably, will be "So what? You still did what you did because it satisfied *your* desires."

The answer to this, of course, is that the desire to help someone else is an unselfish desire, and what is meant by "unselfish act" is precisely an act that is intended to satisfy an unselfish desire.

A second traditional strategy is to clarify that those who hold "we always act selfishly" mean that we always act selfishly *when we act voluntarily,* involuntary acts being beside the point. This clarification having been made, those who hold "we always act selfishly" are in a difficult position. They can establish that we always act selfishly only by defining a selfish act as any act that stems from our desires. Unfortunately, this is also the definition of a voluntary act: a voluntary act by definition is one that we do because we want to; that is, one that stems from our desires. Consequently, the position of those who say "we always act selfishly (when we act voluntarily)" is a mere verbal truism, of no more interest than the claim that a father is always a male. Given their definition of a selfish act, "we always act selfishly when we act voluntarily" really means "our acts always stem from our desires when they stem from our desires."

The reason beginning students find it so difficult to overcome the position of someone who says that we always act selfishly is precisely because that person has been allowed quietly to redefine terms in such a way that an opponent, to win, must refute an analytic truth.

It is hard to find a better illustration of the importance of clarification of terms than in discussion of the notion that we always act selfishly.

24.   *Is it true that moral principles hold without exception? Explain.*

Here we offer some comments regarding how an ethical relativist might respond to this question.

Ethical relativism is a normative theory that holds that people in different societies ought to subscribe only to the standards of their society. (*Cultural* relativism is a nonnormative anthropological or sociological theory, according to which people in different societies subscribe to different moral standards.) Ethical relativists hold, in other words, that your moral judgments are validated or invalidated on the basis of one and only one thing: your society's moral standards.

Several theories that have been called versions of ethical relativism have been proposed in recent years, by Gilbert Harman, David Wong, and others, and there certainly are species of ethical relativism that cannot be summarily dismissed as illogical. Not all these theories preclude cross-cultural evaluation of ethical norms, as does our version of ethical relativism, according to which a society's standards are the highest court of appeal in ethical matters. See M. Krausz and J. Meiland, *Relativism: Cognitive and Moral*, and David B. Wong, *Moral Relativity*.

Beginning philosophy students may be counted on to endorse ethical relativism, as we have set it forth, with enthusiasm. And any philosophical theory that beginning students endorse enthusiastically ought to be subjected to vigorous challenge in an introductory philosophy class.

The standard procedure for challenging the relativistic views of first-semester philosophy students is to invite them to consider the supposed ethical standards of Nazi Germany and ask whether they believe German citizens really should have subscribed to those standards. We are sorry to report that, for whatever reason, our students have not been moved much by this tactic, and are quite prepared to say that German citizens should have done so. They are also quite willing to say that it was not wrong for George Washington to own slaves or for Spartans to abandon deaf babies. Why they are willing to say this we do not know. We only report that it is so.

It has been our experience, however, that if young relativists are asked if the followers of the late Ayatollah Khomeini really should try to assassinate author Salman Rushdie or if Iranian women really should be treated according to the principles of Islamic fundamentalism, they will balk.

Again, why they should balk at these examples and not the earlier ones we cannot say.

However, to get to the main point, can an ethical relativist say that moral principles hold without exception?

To answer this question, a distinction might be made between universal ethical standards and absolute ethical standards. A universal ethical standard is one that all societies do in fact accept. An absolute ethical standard is one that applies to all societies regardless of whether or not they accept it. Our type of ethical relativist will say that there logically could be universal ethical standards, and whether or not there are can only be settled through scientific inquiry. And he or she will also say that if there are, then these also are absolute ethical standards. And finally, he or she will say that, if any ethical standard is absolute, it is only *because* it is universal.

40.   *"There cannot be moral values if there is no God."* *Critically evaluate this assertion.*

Once a visiting instructor of philosophy was asked by a student in an introductory class how anything could be right or wrong if there is no God. His answer was Aristotelian and lengthy and lost everyone. We favor the more streamlined Kantian-type response: "Suppose you claim it is all right for a person not to repay his debts. If your claim were true, there wouldn't be any such thing as a debt. Then what you have maintained is meaningless. Since your claim, if true, is meaningless, your claim is false. Therefore it is not all right for a person not to repay his debts." (Some instructors may regard this as a sophism.)

This question, we wish to note, gives an instructor an excellent opportunity to bring up the old conundrum: Does God command us to do so-and-so because it is right, or is it right to do so-and-so because God commands it? Neither alternative seems to mesh comfortably with Christian beliefs, since the first option seems to place something above God in the ethical chain of command, and the second option seems to make God's commandment arbitrary.

An entire class period can be spent on this conundrum and off-the-cuff student responses to it.

CHAPTER 10

Political Philosophy

Main Points

1. Political philosophy seeks to find the best form of political existence. It is concerned with determining the state's right to exist, its ethically legitimate functions and scope, and its proper organization.

2. Plato and Aristotle

   Plato. **Plato's** *Republic*: the ideal state, analogously to the virtuous person, has three elements (classes—the craftsmen; the police-soldiers; the governing class), each of which fulfills its unique function in accordance with the dictates of reason. Rule and leadership is by an elite subgroup of the guardians, the "philosopher kings."

3. The guardians have neither private property nor private families, and reproduction is controlled so as to improve the bloodline in intelligence, courage, and other leadership qualities.

4. Plato's fivefold classification of the forms of government, each of which after the first is a degeneration of the preceding form: aristocracy, timocracy, plutocracy, democracy, and tyranny.

5. For Plato the state is a living organism whose well-being must be sought by its subjects: a state is good to the extent it is well-ordered.

6. Aristotle. For **Aristotle** too the state is a living organism, one that exists to promote the good life for humans: a state is good to the extent that it enables its citizens to have the good life.

7. Aristotle: The form of the ideal state depends on the circumstances. Proper rule can be by one (monarchy) or by a few (aristocracy) or by the many (polity); improper rule can be by one (tyranny) or by a few (oligarchy) or by the many (democracy). Good forms tend to generate into bad.

8. Aristotle: Inequality among humans is a fact of nature.

9. Despite his descriptivism, Aristotle was not a historian of political systems.

10. <u>Natural Law Theory and Contractarian Theory</u>

    Aristotle is sometimes regarded as the source of natural law political theory, but the clearest conception of natural law is found in Stoic philosophy. **Cicero** gave us the classic expression of Stoic natural law as applied to political philosophy: there is only one valid basis for human law, the natural law of reason, and it holds eternally and universally.

11. <u>Augustine and Aquinas.</u> Both thinkers Christianized natural law as the eternal moral law of God as it is apprehended by humans through the dictates of conscience and reason.

12. Two vital questions raised by Augustine and Aquinas: (1) relationship of secular to natural law; (2) relationship of state to church.

13. Augustine: The purpose of the state is to take the power to do hurt from the wicked; Aquinas: The purpose of the state is to promote the common good.

14. Aquinas's fourfold conception of law: eternal law, divine law, natural law, human law.

15. <u>Hobbes.</u> Natural laws (not law) are rational principles of preservation of life. The first law of nature: seek peace as far as you can and then use any means of defense. The second law: be content, for the sake of peace and self-preservation, with only so much of liberty against others as you would allow them against you. The third law: perform covenants.

16. Applying the foregoing laws of nature to practical affairs leads to the Leviathan through a social contract.

17. There is and can be no contract between the Leviathan and its subjects. This entails: it is impossible for the Leviathan to be unjust; it has the right to lay down any laws it can enforce, although it cannot require suicide; it has no legal or moral obligation to its subjects.

18. If the Leviathan fails to provide security, subjects may transfer power to another sovereign.

19. Hobbes was the first philosopher to enunciate systematically the concept that justice and the state are created through a social contract.

20. Two Other Contractarian Theorists

    John Locke. **Locke's** *Two Treatises of Government* were regarded as the philosophical justification of the Glorious Revolution.

21. Locke: There is a natural moral law that is more than a set of practical principles for survival. Because we are God's, we must seek to preserve ourselves and others: no person can take another's life or impair his life, liberty, health, limbs, or goods except for just punishment.

22. Locke and the right to property. The state is created to protect property and to ensure peace, safety, and the public good. It acquires its legitimacy by an explicit or implicit social contract on the part of its subjects, who entrust their rights to the state for safeguarding.

23. Locke's theory of property implies that all people equally have a right to property, but do not all have a right to equal property.

24. Separation of power. Locke: Only through law are people assured of equal, fair, and impartial treatment and protected from the arbitrary exercise of power by the government. While the lawmaking power is the central power of government, there are two other essential powers: to execute the laws and to make war and peace. Locke recommended the separation of these powers in three branches of government.

25. Though Locke believed it essential that there be a judiciary to settle disputes, the idea that the judiciary should be a separate branch of government belonged to the influential French jurist **Montesquieu.**

26. Jean-Jacques Rousseau. His earliest views notwithstanding, **Rousseau** came to think that through a social contract people give up individual liberty for a superior collective liberty. Through the social contract they create a collective whole or "sovereign," a nonbiological organism that functions according to the general will, which manifests itself by a majority vote and which expresses itself in law.

27. Rousseau: The citizens have the right at any time to terminate the social contract and to depose the official of the state.

28. Did Rousseau establish a philosophical basis for totalitarianism?

29. Mary Wollstonecraft

     Mary Wollstonecraft was annoyed at Rousseau's view of women because he
     advocated that women's education should be designed to make them pleasing to
     men. Wollstonecraft defended the view that society should abandon its practice of
     enculturating women to weakness and dependency.

30. American Constitutional Theory

     Natural law and rights in the Declaration of Independence. The Declaration of
     Independence, in incorporating what had become widespread political theory in the
     American colonies, proclaimed the doctrines of natural law and God-given natural
     rights.

31. Natural law and rights in the U. S. Constitution. The original Constitution refers to
     natural law and rights only implicitly, but its framers regarded the rights of the Bill
     of Rights as the inalienable rights referred to in the Declaration.

32. The right to privacy. An important question today is whether or not the
     Constitution guarantees a right to privacy, and whether or not included within that
     right is a woman's right to abortion.

33. Classic Liberalism and Marxism

     The nineteenth century saw the development of liberal utilitarianism, utopianism,
     and Marxism.

34. Competing utopian theorists, like Claude Saint-Simone, Robert Owen, and Charles
     Fourier, agreed on the social and political equality of women, as did libertarian-
     utilitarians Anna Wheeler, William Thompson, Harriet Taylor, and John Stuart Mill.

35. Harriet Taylor. Taylor and John Stuart Mill (who shared a long personal and
     professional intimacy), along with Mary Wollstonecraft, believed that all differences
     between men and women (excepting, perhaps, some differences in physical
     strength) were socially created.

36. Taylor focused on the concrete issues of women's suffrage and the liberalizing of
     marriage and divorce laws, which, she believed, would produce the greatest
     happiness for the greatest number. She also wrote in defense of minority
     viewpoints, writing that "the opinion of society—majority opinion—is the root of
     all intolerance."

37. John Stuart Mill. **Mill** followed Bentham and Hume in rejecting Locke's theory that
     people have God-given natural rights.

38. Mill, a utilitarian, said that the general happiness—the sum total of happiness of individuals in a group—requires that all enjoy personal liberty to the fullest extent possible consistent with like enjoyment by others. Personal liberty, including freedom of thought and speech, he held, is essential to the general happiness.

39. Mill stated the fundamental principle of liberalism: you cannot interfere with another's liberty for that person's own good but only to prevent harm to others, and the burden of proof lies on the person who claims another's liberty will harm others.

40. Mill: The best form of government is that which among all realistic, practical alternatives produces the greatest benefit. And that, he said, is representative democracy.

41. Mill was sensitive to the threat to liberty in democracies by tyranny of public opinion as well as by suppression of minority points of view.

42. He held that government should not do anything that more effectively can be done privately; nor should government do it, even if it can do it more effectively, if doing it deprives individuals of the opportunity for development or education.

43. <u>From liberalism to Marxism via utopianism.</u> The utopians considered themselves to be implementers of Bentham's utilitarian principle of the greatest happiness for the greatest number. **Saint-Simone** advocated the redistribution of property and social and political power, and love for the poor. **Owen** supported the formation of voluntary work cooperatives where all would share in what was produced. **Fourier** promoted the creation of voluntary associations of individuals living and working in harmonious groups.

44. Utopian philosophers were also important in the struggle for women's rights. In an ideal society, they said, work would be voluntary but people would want to work to improve the community and satisfy their own needs. But the largest, most exploited and only unpaid labor force was women.

45. Utilitarians **Anna Wheeler** and **William Thompson**, in their response to James Mill (the father of John Stuart Mill), wrote against the French doctrine of *couverture* (the idea that women's interests are "covered" by the men who by law are in charge of them, such as fathers, husbands, a male relative, even a son or younger brother). The doctrine provided the basis for denial of legal rights to women.

46. <u>Karl Marx.</u> **Marx:** Said that philosophers have tried only to understand the world, whereas the real point is to change it. He did not regard his work as philosophy.

47. *Means of production versus productive relations.* Marx: The ideal society will lack economic classes, wages, money, private property, and exploitation.

48. It will arise as the result of the dialectical interplay of productive activity and social relationships, which interplay accounts for man's socioeconomic-political situation and also for his morality, law, religion, philosophy, and art.

49. *Class struggle.* According to Marx, the critical social relationships involve property and with the advent of private property, society divided into two classes, those with and those without it.

50. *Capitalism and its consequences.* In modern capitalist societies, according to Marx, production is socialized but ownership of property is not. An inevitable consequence: concentration of wealth into fewer and fewer hands.

51. *Alienation.* The second consequence of continued capitalism is the increasing alienation of workers, who become mere commodities.

52. *Capitalism is self-liquidating.* A further inevitable consequence is the self-liquidation of capitalism: overproduction leading to economic crises and increasingly intolerable conditions for the working class together with increased class self-consciousness will generate a revolution of the working class, leading to a dictatorship of the proletariat, eventually resulting in a classless society.

Boxes

- Plato's Forms of Government
  (Aristocracy, timocracy, plutocracy, democracy, tyranny)

- Aristotle the Political Scientist
  (He was not a neutral describer of political systems)

- War!
  (A discussion of the views of Michael Walzer on when a war is just)

- Aquinas's Conception of Law
  (Eternal law, divine law, natural law, and human law)

- Power Politics: Niccolò Machiavelli
  (Thoughts on The Prince *and* Discourses on Livy*)*

- Profile: Thomas Hobbes

- Profile: John Locke

- Profile: Catharine Trotter Cockburn
  (A stalwart defender of John Locke's philosophy)

- Tacit Consent
  (Our acceptance of the advantages of citizenship provides, as Locke sees it, tacit consent to the state to make and enforce laws)

- The General Will
  (On Rousseau's concept: what is it? how is it determined?)

- Profile: Jean-Jacques Rousseau

- Profile: Mary Wollstonecraft

- Utilitarianism and Natural Rights
  (Utilitarianism seems to require violating "natural rights" if doing so increases the total happiness)

- Adam Smith
  (The notion of the "invisible hand" that promotes the common good)

- Profile: Anna Doyle Wheeler and William Thompson

- Profile: Karl Marx

- Marxism and Liberalism
  (Ten doctrines that many orthodox Marxists accept together with possible classical liberal responses to them)

- Marxism and Communism
  (The difference between Communism and communism)

- Good Marks for Marx on History
  (Calls attention to the idea that economics influences history)

- The Inhuman Condition
  (Under capitalism, says Marxism, a worker does not have full humanness)

- Anarchism
  (A brief discussion of anarchism; mentions Proudhon, Bakunin, and Kropotkin)

Readings

10.1   Thomas Hobbes, from *Leviathan*

This contains the meat of Hobbes's political theory, including his treatment of the state of nature, the first and second natural laws and the right of nature, and his discussion of the causes of commonwealth.

10.2   John Stuart Mill, from *On Liberty*

The famous and stirring "Chapter 1. Introductory" segment of *On Liberty*, in which Mill sets forth the guiding principle of classic liberalism.

10.3   Anne Doyle Wheeler and William Thompson, from *The Appeal of One Half of the Human Race*

A response to James Mill's article on "Government" in the 1814 *Encyclopaedia Britannica Supplement*.

Philosophers' Principal Works

- Plato (c. 427–347 B.C.)
    Republic
    Theaetetus
    Symposium
    Parmenides
    Timaeus
    Apology
    Crito
    Phaedo

- Aristotle (384–322 B.C.)
    Physics
    Metaphysics
    On the Soul (De Anima)
    Nicomachean Ethics
    Politics
    The Organon of logical works

- Cicero (106–43 B.C.)
    On Oratory
    On Duties
    On Fate
    De Re Publica
    De Legibus

- Augustine (354–430)
    Confessions
    De Genesi ad Litteram
    De Trinitate
    The City of God

- Thomas Aquinas (1225–1274)
  On Being and Essence (1253)
  Truth (Quaestiones Disputatae de Veritate [1256–1259])
  Summa Contra Gentiles (1258–1260)
  On the Power of God (1265)
  Summa Theologica (1265–1269)
  In Librum de Causis (1271)

- Thomas Hobbes (1588–1679)
  De Cive (1642)
  De Corpore Politico (1650)
  Leviathan (1651)
  The Questions Concerning Liberty, Necessity, and Chance (1656)
  De Corpore (1665)
  Behemoth (1682)

- Niccolò Machiavelli (1469–1527)
  The Art of War (1521)
  Discourses on Livy (1531)
  The Prince (1532)
  History of Florence (1532)

- John Locke (1632–1704)
  An Essay Concerning Human Understanding (1689)
  Two Treatises of Government (1690)

- Catharine Trotter Cockburn (1679–1749)
  A Defence of Mr. Locke's Essay of Human Understanding

- Charles-Louis de Secondat, baron de Montesquieu (1689–1755)
  Persian Letters (1721)
  The Spirit of the Laws (1748)
  Considerations sur les causes de la grandeur des Romains et de leur decadence (1734)

- Jean-Jacques Rousseau (1712–1778)
  Discourse on the Origin and Foundation of the Inequality among Men (1754)
  Julie, ou la Nouvelle Heloise (1761)
  Émile (1762)
  The Social Contract (1762)
  Confessions (1765–1778)

- Mary Wollstonecraft (1759–1797)
  Thoughts on the Education of Daughters: With Reflections on Female Conduct, in the More Important Duties of Life (1787)
  A Vindication of the Rights of Woman, With Strictures on Political and Moral Subjects (1792)

- Harriet Taylor (1807?–1858)
  The Enfranchisement of Women

- John Stuart Mill (1806–1873)
  A System of Logic (1843)
  On Liberty (1859)
  Utilitarianism (1863)
  The Subjection of Women (1869)
  Autobiography and Literary Essays (1873)

- Adam Smith (1723–1790)
  Theory of Moral Sentiments (1759)
  An Inquiry Into the Nature and Causes of the Wealth of Nations (1776)

- Anna Doyle Wheeler (1785–1848) and William Thompson (1775–1833)
  The Appeal of One Half of the Human Race, Women, Against the Pretensions of the Other Half, Men, to Restrain Them in Political, and Thence in Civil and Domestic, Slavery (1825)

- Claude Saint-Simone (1760–1825)
  The Industrial System (1820)
  The New Christianity (1825)

- Robert Owen (1771–1858)
  A New View of Society, and Other Writings (1813–1821)
  Lectures on an Entire New State of Society (1830)

- Charles Fourier (1772–1837)
  The Theory of Universal Unity (1822)
  The New Industrial and Social World (1829)

- Karl Marx (1818–1883)
  The German Ideology (trans. 1933)
  Communist Manifesto (with Friedrich Engels, 1848)
  Das Capital (volume 1, 1867; volumes 2 and 3, edited by Friedrich Engels, 1885–1894)
  History of Economic Theories (edited by Karl Kautsky, 1952)

- Friedrich Engels (1820–1895)
  The Condition of the Working Class in England in 1844 (1845)
  Communist Manifesto (with Karl Marx, 1848)
  Anti-Dühring (1873)
  The Origin of the Family, Private Property, and the State (1884)
  Socialism, Utopian and Scientific (1883)

- Pierre-Joseph Proudhon (1809–1865)
  What Is Property? (1840)
  System of Economic Contradictions (1846)
  Justice in the Revolution and in the Church (1858)

- Mikhail Bakunin (1814–1876)
  God and the State (trans. 1893)
  Marxism, Freedom, and the State (trans. 1950)

- Piotr Kropotkin (1842–1921)
  Memoirs of a Revolutionist (1899)
  Mutual Aid: A Factor of Evolution (1902)
  Modern Science and Anarchism (1912)
  Ethics (1922)

Lecture-Discussion Ideas Related to Selected Questions

2. *Is the well-being of the state desirable in its own right, apart from what it contributes to the welfare of its citizens?*

If this question were put to them directly, most people would be inclined to answer it negatively, we'd bet. Most probably would have trouble understanding it. And for good reason: it is difficult to attach any precise meaning to the thesis that the well-being of the state is desirable for its own sake and apart from what it contributes to the welfare of its citizens.

Yet the view of the state as an organic entity, the preservation of whose life and health is a desideratum, is implicit in nationalism and imperialism, as well as in such stirringly patriotic slogans as John F. Kennedy's "Ask not what your country can do for you, but what you can do for your country." It is doubtful whether modern wars ever could have been fought in the absence of widespread acceptance of it. It is also evident in the political philosophies of Plato, Rousseau, and Mussolini, but pretty much absent from those of the liberal tradition (Locke, Mill, and so on).

The clearest exposition of the view is in Plato's *Republic*, and also, of course, in Hegel. The following passages should serve to communicate the Hegelian concept to interested students.

"The state is the actuality of the ethical Idea. It is the ethical mind *qua* the substantial will manifest and revealed to itself, knowing and thinking itself, accomplishing what it knows and in so far as it knows it. . . .

"The state is absolutely rational inasmuch as it is the actuality of the substantial will which it possesses in the particular self-consciousness once that consciousness has been raised to consciousness of its universality. This substantial unity is an absolute unmoved end in itself, in which freedom comes into its supreme right. On the other hand this final end has supreme right against the individual, whose supreme duty is to be a member of the state.

"If the state is confused with civil society, and if its specific end is laid down as the security and protection of property and personal freedom, then the interest of the individual as such becomes the ultimate end of their association, and it follows that membership of the state is something optional. But the state's relation to the individual is quite different from this. Since the state is mind objectified, it is only as one of its members that the individual himself has objectivity, genuine individuality, and an ethical life." (Hegel, *Philosophy of Right*, 257–258)

"The rational end of man is life in the state, and if there is no state there, reason at once demands that one be founded. Permission to enter a state or leave it must be given by the state; this then is not a matter which depends on an individual's arbitrary will and therefore the state does not rest on contract, for contract presupposes arbitrariness.

"It is false to maintain that the foundation of the state is something at the option of all its members. It is nearer the truth to say that it is absolutely necessary for every individual to be a citizen." (Hegel, *Philosophy of Right*, Additions, Par. 75)

"We should desire to have in the state nothing except what is an expression of rationality. The state is the world which mind has made for itself; its march, therefore, is on lines that are fixed and absolute. How often we talk of the wisdom of God in nature! But we are not to assume for that reason that the physical world of nature is a loftier thing than the world of mind.

"As high as mind stands above nature, so high does the state stand above physical life. Man must therefore venerate the state as a secular deity, and observe that if it is difficult to comprehend nature, it is infinitely harder to understand the state." (Hegel, *Philosophy of Right*, Additions, Par. 272)

3. *Evaluate Aristotle's idea that people who do not have the aptitude or time to participate in governance should not be citizens.*

Here is Aristotle's analysis of "citizen":

"Who is the citizen, and what is the meaning of the term? . . . We may say, first, that a citizen is not a citizen because he lives in a certain place, for resident aliens and slaves share in the place; nor is he a citizen who has no legal right except that of suing and being sued; for this right may be enjoyed under the provisions of a treaty. . . . The citizen whom we are seeking to define is a citizen in the strictest sense, against whom no such exception can be taken, and his special characteristic is that he shares in the administration of justice, and in offices. . . . He who has the power to take part in the deliberative or judicial administration of any state is said by us to be a citizen of that state; and, speaking generally, a state is a body of citizens sufficing for the purposes of life." (*Politics*, 1274b38)

So, roughly, Aristotle defined a citizen as one who shares in the administration of justice, from which definition it follows analytically that those who, for whatever reasons, do not or cannot do so cannot be citizens. Aristotle also thought that mechanics and tradesmen lead lives inimical to virtue and that husbandmen do not have the time either to develop virtue or to perform political duties; and that consequently members of these three classes are not fit for citizenship in the well-governed state:

"[T]he citizens must not lead the life of mechanics or tradesmen, for such a life is ignoble and inimical to virtue. Neither must they be husbandmen, since leisure is necessary for the development of virtue and the performance of political duties. . . . Besides, the ruling class should be the owners of property, for they are citizens, and the citizens of a state should be in good circumstances; whereas mechanics or any other class which is not a producer of virtue have no share in the state. This follows from our first principle, for happiness cannot exist without virtue, and a city is not to be termed happy in regard to a portion of the citizens, but in regard to them all. And clearly property should be in their hands, since the husbandmen will of necessity be slaves or barbarian *Perioeci.*" (*Politics*, 1328b33)

CHAPTER 11

Recent Moral and Political Philosophy

Main Points

1. Analytic ethical philosophy is often said to begin with **G. E. Moore**, who believed that the task of the philosopher of ethics is to conduct a "general inquiry into what is good."

2. G. E. Moore

    Moore: Good is a noncomplex (undefinable, unanalyzable) and nonnatural property of good things.

3. Moore's opinion about what things are good is of less importance than his metaethical opinions.

4. Metaethics is the philosophical investigation into the logical relationships of moral value judgments, or into the sources, criteria, meaning, verification, or validation of moral value judgments. It is distinct from normative ethics, which consists of making and defending moral value judgements. Much contemporary analytic ethical philosophy has been metaethical.

5. W. D. Ross

    Ross examined the nature, relations, and implications of three fundamental conceptions in ethics: "right," "good" in general, and "morally good."

6. Ross: The production of good is not the sole thing that makes an act right; there are prima facie (not absolute) duties—things it is our duty to do unless that duty is overridden by some other duty.

7. Ross: Some true moral propositions are self-evident truths.

8. <u>Emotivism and Beyond</u>

   Common ground among the utilitarians, Moore, and Ross: moral judgments are a type of factual judgment.

9. The emotivists (e.g., **C. L. Stevenson**) held that moral judgments have no factual meaning, but are linguistic acts by which a speaker expresses an attitude about something or other.

10. Many analytic philosophers thought that the emotivist analysis of moral judgments was not correct. **R. M. Hare**: The function of moral discourse is to guide conduct. A moral judgment is a universalizable prescriptive judgment.

11. The so-called "naturalist fallacy," adopted by many moral philosophers in the first half of the twentieth century, reflected Hume's view that one cannot deduce an "ought" from an "is." But now, many philosophers, including **Phillipa Foot** and **John Searle**, no longer accept the idea that moral evaluations are logically independent of the descriptive premises they are based on.

12. The rejection of emotivism, and the idea that there are empirical criteria for moral evaluations, have spurred a renewed interest in concrete ethical issues, such as sexual morality, affirmative action, biomedical ethics, business ethics, and the environment.

13. Though metaethics is not dead, it is true that many ethics courses focus increasingly on questions of applied ethics.

14. **James Rachels** discusses whether it is really true that letting people die of starvation is as bad as killing them.

15. <u>John Rawls, A Contemporary Liberal</u>

   The work of contractarian theorist **John Rawls** in social and political philosophy heralded a renewed concern in philosophy with justice.

16. <u>The fundamental requirements of the just society.</u> Rawls: If society is to be well-ordered, its members must determine by rational reflection what are to be their principles of justice; the principles must be selected by a fair procedure.

17. <u>The veil of ignorance and the original position.</u> In the selection of principles of justice, no one should have insider's knowledge so that no one is advantaged or disadvantaged in the choice of principles by his or her unique circumstances. The principles are chosen as if from behind a veil of ignorance; this what Rawls calls the original position or initial situation.

18. The two principles of social justice. These are the principles that would be selected in the original position: (1) Each person has an equal right to "the most extensive basic liberty compatible with a similar liberty for others." (2) Social and economic inequalities must be arranged "so that they are both (a) reasonably expected to be to everyone's advantage and (b) attached to positions and offices open to all."

19. The priority of (1) over (2) dictates that a person's liberty cannot be sacrificed for the common good.

20. The rights of individuals. Rawls in effect attempts to derive social ethics from a basis in rational self-interest rather from God, natural law, human nature, utility, or other ground.

21. Why should I accept that? Rawls's theory, if correct, specifies the fundamental principles of social justice that self-interested but rational people would accept on reflection.

22. In *Political Liberalism*, published in 1993, Rawls considers more closely how "justice as fairness" can be endorsed by the members of a pluralistic democratic society (who hold incompatible religious and philosophical doctrines). He characterizes justice more narrowly than he did earlier, as a freestanding political conception and not as a comprehensive value system.

23. Political justice becomes the focus of an overlapping consensus of comprehensive value systems and thus can still be embraced by all in a pluralistic democratic society.

24. Robert Nozick's Libertarianism

    Nozick's *Anarchy, State, and Utopia* asked a basic question: Should there even be a political state, and if so, why?

25. A minimal state is justified. Only a minimal state limited to the narrow functions of protection against force, theft, fraud, enforcement of contracts, and so on, is justified.

26. Only the "night-watchman" state does not violate rights. Any state more powerful or extensive than the minimal state that protects its citizens from force and fraud and the like impinges on the individual's natural rights to his or her holdings and therefore is not legitimate.

27. This is based on Nozick's "entitlement" concept of social justice that says a person is entitled to what he or she has rightfully acquired, and justice consists in each person's retaining control over his or her rightful acquisitions.

28. <u>The rights of individuals.</u> Nozick's assertion that individuals have rights (including property rights) may have something to do with the presumed inviolability of individuals that prohibits their being used as means to ends, and perhaps also with the necessary conditions for allowing them to give meaning to their lives, but its justification is unclear.

29. <u>Communitarian Responses to Rawls</u>

    Communitarian critics of Rawls, such as **Michael Sandel**, **Michael Walzer**, and **Alasdair MacIntyre**, hold that the "common good" is defined by one's society or "community." Sandel believes the community is an intersubjective or collective "self" and that the Rawlsian principle of equal liberty is subordinate to the good of this social organism.

30. Sandel: The community is an intersubjective or collective self because self-understanding comprehends more than just an individual human being; the Rawlsian principle of equal liberty is subordinate to the good of this social organism.

31. Walzer: Any full account of how social goods ought to be distributed will be "thick," framed within this or that specific political association or "culture." Principles of abstract justice are oversimplifications, which themselves reflect particular cultural viewpoints.

32. <u>Alasdair MacIntyre and virtue ethics.</u> For virtue ethics, traits of character are in many ways more fundamental than rules for action.

33. In *After Virtue*, MacIntyre says that "there is no way to possess the virtues except as part of a tradition in which we inherit them and our understanding of them from a series of predecessors."

34. MacIntyre (and Aristotle): Virtues are traits that promote human flourishing.

35. For MacIntyre, Nietzsche (with his call to "raze to the ground the structures of inherited moral belief and argument") represents the ultimate alternative to Aristotle.

36. MacIntyre emphasized the "concept of a self whose unity resides in the unity of a narrative which links birth to life to death as narrative beginning to middle to end." A particular action viewed outside the context of a person's life is unintelligible; each person's quest for his or her own good or excellence must be undertaken from within that person's moral tradition.

37. MacIntyre: A virtue may be analyzed as a quality required to attain a good internal to a practice. To understand the human good we can rank the goods internal to human practices.

38. (Note: MacIntyre himself has disavowed the "communitarian" label since the attempt to institute communitarian principles in a large nation state may well result in tyranny.)

39. Feminist Thought

Feminist thought is often divided into two "waves": from the late eighteenth century through about 1922 (when women in the United States received the right to vote); and from 1949 (with the publication of Simone de Beauvoir's *The Second Sex*) to the present.

40. The first wave focused on legal issues; the second wave (often referred to as feminism) focused on personal issues, especially the personal relations between men and women.

41. **Mary Wollstonecraft** painted an unflattering portrait of the "ideal" woman of her era, suggesting that women who have no other ambition than to inflame passions will have no real strength of character.

42. **Harriet Taylor**: The nonphysiological differences between men and women were socially constructed. She argued that we cannot make arbitrary distinctions between groups of people without giving good reasons for doing so, and that no good reasons could be given for saying that men could vote and women could not.

43. **Simone de Beauvoir** brought to feminist thought the Continental traditions of existentialism and phenomenology. Her focus was on the cultural mechanisms of oppression that left women in the role of the Other to man's Self.

44. Reflecting her existentialist concerns, de Beauvoir believed that despite cultural, social, and political conditioning, and the deterministic conclusions of Freud and Marx, one could always recreate herself anew and transcend the straitjacket of any given culture.

45. De Beauvoir argues that "one is not born, but rather becomes, a woman." That is, the category "woman" is another name for "Other" and is imposed by a male-dominated society, just as neighbors tend to treat strangers as "Other."

46. She emphasized the activity of the mind as the distinctly human activity, so that a woman's "free" choice to stay at home and have babies is really a kind of dehumanization.

47. **Kate Millett** examined domination and subordination in a society, and the consequences for women of being born into a patriarchal society (as most societies are and have been).

48. Androgyny as an alternative. Many feminists in the late 1960s and early 1970s thought that an androgynous society would, in its homogeneity, eliminate the Other versus Self division.

49. **Ann Ferguson** endorsed monoandrogyny, in which both girls and boys were raised exactly the same. Ideal love, which is a love between equals, would then be possible.

50. **Joyce Trebilcot** endorsed polyandrogyny, in which the concepts of feminine and masculine were kept alive but were not always matched up with women and men respectively: Men would be free to choose to be "feminine" men; women would be free to choose to be "masculine" women, and no social stigma would be attached to any such choice. (Such a society might freely chose monoandrogyny.)

51. Problems with androgyny as an ideal. Some feminist theorists questioned the viability of androgyny, and whether (and how) such "masculine" traits as rationality and competition could be combined with such "feminine" traits as expression of inner feelings and the role of nurturer.

52. **Marilyn Frye** argues that the whole system of gender is really one of power: masculinity is about dominance, femininity about subordination. A culture that maintains gender differences as a mask for the oppression of women is inherently sexist.

53. Feminist moral theory. Researcher **Carol Gilligan** argues that studies of moral development in childhood tend to be studies of boys. Gilligan maintains that girls put more emphasis on care and the preservation of personal relationships while boys put more emphasis on abstract justice and individual rights. Context and care for others are central features in women's moral reasoning.

54. Psychoanalyst **Nancy Chodorow** argues that contemporary child-rearing practices foster a strong need for connectedness in little girls and for separation and autonomy in little boys. Thus, girls and boys learn very different lessons about how to relate to the world and others in it.

55. **Nel Noddings**: An ethics of care is not a set of principles or maxims but a way of responding to people and situations. (Noddings, unlike Gilligan, believes the ethics of care preferable to an ethics of rights; Gilligan does not make this claim of superiority.)

56. **Sara Ruddick**: "Maternal thinking" puts a priority on "holding" over "acquiring" and is distinguished from the "instrumentalism of technocracy." Ruddick also warns against sentimentalizing the maternal virtues of "humility" and "cheerfulness."

57. Some feminist ethicists have noted that a care-centered ethics has perhaps not been freely chosen by women, but has arisen to serve the needs of patriarchal society. Other feminist writers have emphasized the utility of an ethics of rights and justice as a foundation for social institutions where the competing claims of persons who do not know each other must be balanced.

58. *Justice, Gender, and the Family:* Susan Moller Okin. A person's gender is the person's biological sex as constructed, understood, interpreted, and institutionalized by society.

59. **Okin**: The theories of Rawls, Nozick, MacIntyre, Walzer, Sandel, and others have been virtually blind to questions of justice raised by the facts of gender.

60. Okin: Nozick's theory is nonsense since it rests on the belief that each person owns himself; but that assumption only works if it is ignored that persons are themselves products of specifically female capacities and female labor. Under Nozick's theory that a person owns what he produces and such entitlement takes precedence over all other rights, "women's entitlement rights to those they produce must take priority over persons' rights to themselves at birth." It follows that persons do not own themselves and there is no basis for them owning anything else either.

61. Okin: MacIntyre's ethical "traditions," which, according to him, give the best account of justice, not only exclude but depend "upon the exclusion of the great majority of people, including all women." In the tradition MacIntyre favors, that constituted by Plato, Aristotle, Augustine, and Thomas Aquinas, woman is seen as a deformity in nature and the blame for men's sinful lust.

62. Okin: Rawls's two principles of justice "can lead us to challenge fundamentally the gender system of our society." Fulfilling Rawls's criteria for justice would require abolition of gender. But Rawls is faulted for simply assuming the family is a just institution.

63. Okin: The practices of family life in society today are structured by gender, which makes women vulnerable. The "cycle of inequality is perpetuated" as the difference between the wages wives make in the workforce and their husbands' wages increases over time.

64. Herbert Marcuse, a Contemporary Marxist

    Marcuse: Members of the working class, instead of being disenfranchised, have been integrated into advanced capitalistic society.

65. Their needs have been satisfied, but they have lost their capacity to choose and act for themselves, to refuse, to dissent, to create, to think.

66. And the needs are false needs, whose satisfaction promotes wastefulness and fails to lead to fulfillment of the individual or release from domination.

67. Consequently, the workers have become a force for preserving the status quo.

68. Society has become one-dimensional: labor and capital have been unified against Communism in a welfare and warfare state; art, language, philosophy, and science have lost their original creative and critical power.

69. But in his later thought Marcuse perceived a weakening of the immersion of the working class into capitalist society, and a growing awareness of workers, students, and the middle class of the high price of consumer prosperity. Through a revolution born not of privation but of reaction against waste and excess, a society without war, exploitation, poverty, and waste still might come.

Boxes

- Six Biggies
  (We distinguish six basic types of ethical theory: divine-command, consequentialist, deontological, virtue ethics, relativism, and contractarianism)

- Normative Ethics and Metaethics
  (Explains the difference between first-order thinking and second-order thinking)

- Losing Sight of the Big Issues?
  (Why metaethics isn't guilty of this)

- Values Without God
  (If there is no God is everything permissible?)

- Current Controversies in Metaethics
  (Is there a distinction, for example, between morally obligatory acts and supererogatory acts?)

- Environmental Philosophy
  (What are the philosophical root causes of ecological crises? What entities have moral standing and intrinsic value?)

- Twentieth-Century Isms
  (Liberalism, conservatism, Communism, communism, socialism, capitalism, fascism—these ill-defined terms do not stand for parallel alternative forms of government. Edmund Burke is mentioned.)

- Political Trends
  (On modern political movements)

- Self-Respect
  (The most important good, according to Rawls)

- Invisible Hand Explanations
  (Nozick explains how the state came about)

- Animals and Morality
  (Nozick on the status of animals and a brief discussion of animal rights)

- Robin Hood
  (Nozick's, Rawls's, and a utilitarian's views)

- Virtue Ethics
  (Modern interpreters of the virtue ethics tradition of Plato, Aristotle, and Aquinas)

- Profile: Simone de Beauvoir

- Profile: Gloria Steinem

- Shulamith Firestone: Biology and Oppression
  (Firestone argued that women's capacity for childbirth was one main source of their oppression, and that new reproductive technologies needed to be developed)

- I See By Your Outfit That You Are a Feminist
  (Considers the question of the role of clothing in women's oppression)

- Liberal Feminism and Radical Feminism
  (Briefly considers the differences between these two strategies for women's liberation)

- The Strategy of Separatism
  (Some feminists have argued that living apart from their oppressors will provide them with strength and solidarity)

- Women and Violence
  (Some disturbing statistics about domestic—and other—violence)

- Why Should Women Have a Voice in Government?
  (The classic answer provided by Harriet Taylor)

- Marcuse in Southern California
  (A brief account of Marcuse's difficulties in conservative San Diego)

Readings

11.1   John Rawls, from *A Theory of Justice*

In this selection Rawls gives an overview of the major aspects of his book.

11.2   Robert Nozick, from *Anarchy, State, and Utopia*

This is a "side discussion" in Nozick's book, but it is interesting and worthwhile. In it Nozick criticizes a principle of fairness that most beginning students in philosophy would probably be inclined to accept.

11.3   Susan Moller Okin, from *Justice, Gender, and the Family*

Okin argues that "the combined effect of the omission of the family and the falsely gender-neutral language in recent political thought is that most theorists are continuing to ignore the highly political issue of gender." She also addresses the central importance of families in teaching justice, and draws on the thought of John Rawls in contrasting the characteristics of a just family with those unjust characteristics of current gender-based structures and practices.

11.4   Nel Noddings, from *Caring: A Feminine Approach to Ethics and Moral Education*

"The source of ethical behavior is . . . in twin sentiments—one that feels directly for the other and one that feels for and with the best self, who may accept and sustain the initial feeling rather than reject it." Noddings also discusses the nature of ethical obligation, which, she says, "is limited and delimited by relation." ("Universal love," she writes, "is illusion.")

Philosophers' Principal Works

- G. E. Moore (1873–1958)
  Principia Ethics (1903)
  "The Refutation of Idealism" (1903)
  Ethics (1912)
  Some Main Problems of Philosophy (1953)
  Philosophical Papers (1959)

- W. D. Ross (1877–1970)
  Plato's Theory of Ideas (1951)
  The Right and the Good (1930)
  Foundations of Ethics (1939)

- C. L. Stevenson (1908–1979)
  Ethics and Language (1944)
  Facts and Values (1963)
  Values and Morals (1978)

- R. M. Hare (1919–)
  The Language of Morals (1952)
  Freedom and Reason (1964)
  Essays on the Moral Concepts (1972)
  Essays on Philosophical Method (1972)
  Practical Inferences (1972)

- Phillipa Foot (1920–)
    "Moral Arguments" (1958)
    "Moral Beliefs" (1958)
    Virtues and Vices (1978)
    Theories of Ethics (1990)

- John Searle (1932–)
    Intentionality: An Essay in the Philosophy of Mind (1983)
    Minds, Brains, and Science: The 1984 Reith Lectures (1984)
    The Rediscovery of the Mind (1992)
    The Construction of Social Reality (1995)
    The Mystery of Consciousness (1997)

- James Rachels (1941–)
    The Elements of Moral Philosophy (1986)
    The End of Life: Euthanasia and Morality (1986)

- John Rawls (1921–)
    A Theory of Justice (1971)
    Political Liberalism (1993)

- Robert Nozick (1938–)
    Anarchy, State, and Utopia (1974)
    Philosophical Explanations (1981)
    The Nature of Rationality (1993)

- Michael Sandel (1953–)
    Liberalism and the Limits of Justice (1982)
    Democracy's Discontent: American In Search of a Public Philosophy (1996)

- Michael Walzer (1935–)
    Spheres of Justice: A Defense of Pluralism and Equality (1983)
    Thick and Thin, Moral Arguments at Home and Abroad (1994)
    On Toleration (1997)

- Alasdair MacIntyre (1929–)
    After Virtue (1981)
    Whose Justice? Which Rationality? (1988)
    Three Rival Versions of Moral Enquiry (1990)

- Mary Wollstonecraft (1759–1797)
    Thoughts on the Education of Daughters: With Reflections on Female Conduct, in the More Important Duties of Life (1787)
    A Vindication of the Rights of Woman, With Strictures on Political and Moral Subjects (1792)

- Harriet Taylor (1807?–1858)
    The Enfranchisement of Women

- Simone de Beauvoir (1908–1986)
  The Second Sex (1953)
  Memoirs of a Dutiful Daughter (1959)
  The Prime of Life (1962)

- Gloria Steinem (1934–)
  Outrageous Acts and Everyday Rebellions (1983)
  Revolution From Within: A Book of Self-Esteem (1992)
  Moving Beyond Words (1994)

- Kate Millett (1934–)
  Sexual Politics (1970)

- Ann Ferguson (1938–)
  Blood at the Root: Motherhood, Sexuality, and Male Dominance (1989)
  Sexual Democracy: Women, Oppression, and Revolution (1991)

- Joyce Trebilcot (1933–)
  Mothering: Essays in Feminist Theory (ed.) (1983)
  Dyke Ideas: Process, Politics, and Daily Life (1994)

- Marilyn Frye (1941–)
  The Politics of Reality: Essays in Feminist Theory (1983)
  Willful Virgin (1992)

- Carol Gilligan (1936–)
  In a Different Voice: Psychological Theory and Women's Development (1982)
  Making Connections: The Relational Worlds of Adolescent Girls at Emma Willard School (joint author) (1990)

- Nancy Chodorow (1944–)
  The Reproduction of Mothering: Psychoanalysis and the Sociology of Gender (1978)
  Feminism and Psychoanalysis (1989)
  Femininities, Masculinities, Sexualities: Freud and Beyond (1994)

- Nel Noddings (1929–)
  Caring: A Feminine Approach to Ethics and Moral Education (1984)

- Sara Ruddick (1935–)
  Maternal Thinking: Towards a Politics of Peace (1990)

- Susan Moller Okin
  Women in Western Political Thought (1980)
  Justice, Gender, and the Family (1989)

- Herbert Marcuse (1898–1979)
    Reason and Revolution (1960)
    One-Dimensional Man (1964)
    Eros and Civilization (1966)
    An Essay on Liberation (1966)
    Negations (1968)

- Edmund Burke (1729–1797)
    A Vindication of Natural Society (1756)
    Philosophical Inquiry Into the Origin of Our Ideas On the Sublime and the Beautiful (1756)
    Reflections on the Revolution in France (1790)

Lecture-Discussion Ideas Related to Selected Questions

11. *Can you think of an ethical principle that would prohibit the killing, hurting, sacrificing, or eating of humans for the sake of other ends that would not equally pertain to animals?*

Well, one principle that would work is, "It is okay to hurt, sacrifice, and eat animals but not humans."

This, of course, is not the sort of principle we had in mind.

When we ask our students to justify medical experimentation on animals, the answers we get are usually these, listed in no particular order:

1. Without medical experimentation on animals, we wouldn't have vaccines for polio and rabies, treatments for whiplash, and so on.

2. Humans are higher on the evolutionary ladder.

3. Humans can reason.

4. Humans are made in the image of God.

5. God created animals to serve people.

6. Animals don't have souls.

7. Animals themselves benefit from medical experimentation on animals.

8. Laboratory animals wouldn't have had the chance to live in the first place if they hadn't been bred for medical experiments.

These answers are easily disposed of, of course. 1 is false, because we could still experiment on other humans, and 1 doesn't explain why we shouldn't experiment on humans. 2, the favorite of many medical researchers, doesn't have any clear meaning and in any case doesn't by itself justify experimenting on creatures who are "lower" on the ladder. 3 is not true of all humans. 4 is at best only a metaphorical usage of "image" that has no clear meaning. 5: How does this fact, if it is a fact, justify experimentation on animals? If 6 is true, it gives us all the more reason to treat animals carefully in this life, since without souls animals cannot have an afterlife. The reasoning employed in 7 would also justify running medical experiments on humans. 8: So it would be okay to experiment on humans as long as we bred them for that purpose?

More sophisticated defenses of medical experimentation on animals usually take one or another of these forms:

- Utilitarian defense—the greatest happiness of the greatest number justifies medical experimentation on animals.

- Contractarian defense—animals could not be party to a social contract in terms of which alone there can be ethical values.

- Natural-rights defense—only humans have rights.

The rejoinders to these are that the utilitarian defense would justify experimenting on certain humans; the contractarian defense does not by itself justify experimenting on creatures that could not be party to a social contract, and if it did, it would also justify experimenting on humans who could not be party; and the natural-rights defense leaves the important work unexplained, why humans alone have natural rights.

Ultimately, students who defend medical experimentation on animals will state something to the effect that human lives are just inherently worth more than animal lives. This claim, however, even if true, does not by itself justify medical experimentation on animals, though it might justify saving this human over saving that animal, if the hard choice must be made. Human life's being more valuable than animal life is perhaps a necessary condition of medical experimentation on animals, but it isn't a sufficient condition.

23.   *Do all oppressed groups suffer? Are all groups that suffer oppressed?*

You can draw on the work of Marilyn Frye for a response to this question. It's important to emphasize to students that Frye thinks that "suffering" and "oppression" are different.

This subject frequently comes up in the discussion of feminist issues. Students will argue—correctly—that white men suffer in their lives. Frye suggests that simple suffering is not sufficient for oppression; indeed, oppressors (as her rich-white-male-South African-playboy example shows) can suffer pretty dismally. But if their options are not systematically limited by the social structures under which they live, then they do not count as oppressed.

Nor does being oppressed necessarily manifest itself as suffering. There are plenty of historical cases of people who were abjectly oppressed (certain slaves, for instance) who did not experience themselves as suffering. Nevertheless, because they labored under social structures that systematically immobilized them and limited their opportunities, Frye would argue that they were oppressed.

Oppression, in short, is more objective than suffering. Suffering requires that the individual feel some sort of psychological discomfort and that the individual be aware of that discomfort. Oppression has to do with the social system that surrounds all members of the community and that systematically advantages one group and disadvantages another. It follows from this analysis that one can be oppressed without knowing it, whereas one cannot suffer without knowing it.

29. *Critically discuss Marcuse's theory that the needs satisfied by advanced capitalist societies are to a large extent false needs.*

On the first day of the semester one of us noticed that a girl out in the second row had *green hair*. That, he was inclined to think, is a false need if there ever was one.

But is it? Probably the need for green hair is the result of a rather complicated set of psychological factors, and, really, there is no clear sense in which those factors—or the needs they generate—are false.

That's the difficulty with the idea that some needs are false. There really aren't any clear criteria for evaluating needs as false or . . . well, just what is the alternative? True? Genuine? Legitimate?

Maybe, to say that a need is a false need is just to express your distaste for it. Maybe it is to insinuate that, like a Tchaikovsky symphony, it doesn't quite measure up, that it is a need that cultured, sensitive people, people like you and us, just don't have, or at least don't indulge. Maybe a false need just is one you would be *embarrassed* to admit to having. It would be one that shows everyone that you have *bad taste*.

All in all we find the idea of false needs obscure. Any definition we might propose for the idea will, in all probability, suffer from the same vagueness as the idea itself. There also aren't any need-experts around that we can turn to for the criteria of legitimacy of need. And it obviously won't help to attempt to derive such criteria by scrutinizing the needs that society itself recognizes.

Followers of Epicurus might try to ground the concept of a false need in human nature. We may suppose that they would classify some needs as natural and necessary (to satisfy), others as natural but not necessary, and still others as neither necessary nor natural, and would regard as false needs all that do not fall into the first group.

But it is questionable how far this strategy will carry us. Your need for a second BMW doesn't seem natural or necessary to me. But to you, given the kind of job you have and the kind of people you must impress, the second BMW is necessary and your need for it is at least as natural as the need for anything else that exceeds the requirements of bare subsistence.

On the other hand, advanced capitalist societies do have the reputation of developing new products and then creating a need for those products through clever advertising. Usually, though, the need isn't developed by advertisers out of whole cloth. Usually the new product arguably will make life more comfortable or pleasant or secure or interesting in some way or other—though it might take some effort to convince people of this—or at the least will respond to people's needs to be accepted or liked or in style. There are, of course, exceptions.

Striped toothpaste, for example, probably responds to no need other than that of the manufacturer to differentiate his product from the other brands.

All in all, we are inclined to think that the concept of a false need is not generally a very useful concept. It is better, we think, just to point out that some needs are better left unsatisfied. A need that is injurious to one's own health, happiness, or long-range well-being, for example, is better left unsatisfied. A need that, if satisfied, tends to promote the destruction of the environment—such as the need to use Styrofoam cups—is better left unsatisfied. So is a need that unnecessarily wastes resources. So is a need that can be satisfied only at the expense of other people, or other living things. Any need that is pathological probably ought not be satisfied either, though the need ought to be removed.

On the whole we think discussion of this question might do well to focus on what sorts of needs ought not be satisfied, and why; and on which of the needs we have actually fall into that category.

CHAPTER 12

Philosophy and Belief in God

Main Points

1. Religious commitment involves philosophical beliefs. The philosophy of religion attempts to understand and rationally evaluate these beliefs. In contrast to theology, it does not make religious assumptions in doing so.

2. The beliefs of the Judeo-Christian religious tradition have received the most discussion by Western philosophers.

3. Two Christian Greats

    Anselm. Though he thought it impossible for anyone to reason about God or God's existence without already believing in him, **Anselm** was willing to evaluate on its own merit and independently of religious assumptions the idea that God does *not* exist.

4. *The ontological argument.* Anselm's ontological arguments attempt to show that disbelief in God entails self-contradiction.

5. *Gaunilo's objection.* **Gaunilo** attempted to refute Anselm's first argument, using the idea of the most perfect island. If Anselm's reasoning is sound, Gaunilo argued, then the most perfect island must exist in reality since if it didn't, any island that did exist in reality would be more perfect than the most perfect island.

6. Aquinas. **Aquinas's** Five Ways: the first three proofs of God's existence (motion, causation, contingency) are versions of cosmological argument; the fourth proof (degrees of goodness) is a moral argument; the fifth proof (purpose) is a teleological argument. Many consider the third way the soundest proof; Aquinas favored the first way.

7. *The first way.* Because there is change in general, a first mover (God) must therefore exist that is moved by no other.

8. *The second way.* Nothing causes itself; if no first cause exists, there would be no effects. So we must admit a first cause, namely, God. For Aquinas, there cannot be an infinite series of simultaneous causes or movers.

9. *The third way.* If everything belonged to the category "need not exist," then at one time nothing existed. That being the case, nothing would exist now. Thus, there must be something the existence of which is necessary, and since it is impossible to go on to infinity in necessary things that have their necessity caused by another, there must be a necessary being that has its own necessity, and this is God.

10. *The fourth and fifth ways.* All natural things possess degrees of goodness, truth, and all other perfections; there must be that which is the source of these perfections, and that is what is called God. Natural things act for an end or purpose, functioning in accordance with a plan or design; thus, an intelligent being exists by which things are directed toward their end, and this intelligent being is God.

11. <u>Mysticism</u>

    It is one thing to say "God came to me" in mystical experience, but another to explain why such experience is a reliable form of knowledge.

12. The mystic **Julian of Norwich** focuses on the nature of personal religious and moral knowledge, as well as on whether it is possible to know God. She denied that there is any meaningful difference in the validity of mystical revelations (she called them "showings") made directly to our soul and knowledge derived through reason. We can know God only partly through revelation; further knowledge comes through loving God.

13. For Julian, God lives in us and we in God; we are one with God and are nurtured and fed knowledge of God and of ourselves by this divine parent.

14. Julian: The knowledge God gives the mystics can provide reasons for ordinary people to have hope in the midst of wars, plagues, and religious disputes.

15. <u>Seventeenth-Century Perspectives</u>

    <u>Descartes.</u> **Descartes** found God's existence indubitable, for three reasons. The first two are combination ontological-cosmological arguments; the third is a streamlined ontological argument.

16. *Descartes's first proof.* Descartes reasons that he is a thinking thing who finds within his mind the idea of God, of an infinite and perfect being. There must be a cause of such an idea, but because there must be as much reality or perfection in the cause of an idea as there is in the content of the idea, God exists.

17. *Descartes's second proof.* (1) I exist as a thing that has an idea of God; (2) everything that exists has a cause that brought it into existence and that sustains it in existence; (3) the only thing adequate to cause and sustain me, a thing that has an idea of God, is God; (4) therefore God exists.

18. It seems possible to devise alternative explanations for one's having the idea of God; Descartes's first proofs depend on this not being possible.

19. *Descartes's third proof.* A version of the ontological argument: (1) My conception of God is the conception of a being that possesses all perfections; (2) existence is a perfection; (3) therefore I cannot conceive of God as not existing; (4) God therefore exists.

20. Leibniz. **Leibniz** employed the principle of sufficient reason to prove God: unless there is something outside the series of events, some reason for the entire series itself, there is no sufficient reason for any occurrence.

21. The proof is thought by many to be the soundest cosmological argument.

22. Eighteenth-Century Perspectives

    Hume. His criticism of the teleological argument (argument from design): We cannot attribute to the cause any qualities beyond those, or different from those, required for the effect; given the limitedness of our viewpoint we cannot say that the world is perfect or deserves praise; we cannot infer cause from a single effect; we cannot assume that the cause of the world is like the causes of happenings in it or that the entire world was created by the same mechanisms by which happenings in it are caused; we cannot be sure the world is not the result of trial and error by a multitude of creators; we are in no position to evaluate the comparison of the world to a human artifact.

23. Hume's criticisms of the cosmological argument, which concludes that a necessary being, an uncaused cause, exists: (1) As far as we can make out, the universe may itself be "the necessarily existing being"; (2) if you maintain that everything has a prior cause it is contradictory also to maintain that there was a first cause; (3) if I explain the cause of each member of a series of things there is no further need for an explanation of the series itself as if it were some further thing.

24. Kant. Provided one of the most famous moral arguments for God's existence, but criticized the three traditional proofs.

25. *What is wrong with the ontological proof?* The ontological argument assumes that existence is a predicate, which is false.

26. *What is wrong with the cosmological and teleological proofs?* The cosmological argument rests on the ontological argument, and employs a principle (that every contingent has a cause) that has significance only in experience, to arrive at a conclusion beyond experience. The teleological argument, according to Kant, proves at best only an architect who works with the matter in the world, and not a creator.

27. *Belief in God rationally justified.* Nevertheless, although we do not have theoretical or metaphysical proof of God, God's existence must be assumed as a postulate of practical reason.

28. <u>Nineteenth-Century Perspectives</u>

    <u>Newman.</u> Offered an argument for God based on the fact of conscience: There is no logical proof that God exists, but concrete or real-life reasoning finds certitude in the feelings of conscience that we are answerable to an intelligence beyond ourselves.

29. <u>Kierkegaard.</u> For **Kierkegaard**, God is beyond the grasp of reason and the idea that God came to us as a man in the person of Jesus is intellectually absurd; yet Kierkegaard was totally committed to Christianity.

30. Kierkegaard: Truth is subjective; it lies not in what we believe, but in how we live. We must commit ourselves to God not through a search for objective truth (there isn't any) but through a leap of faith, through a nonintellectual, passionate, commitment to Christianity.

31. Kierkegaard: The objective uncertainty of God is essential to a true faith in Him.

32. <u>Nietzsche.</u> When **Nietzsche** writes that "God is dead," he does not mean that God once existed and now no longer does. He means instead that there is no intelligent plan to the universe and the order we imagine to exist is merely pasted on by the human mind. But the mass of people, motivated mainly by resentment, see the world as law-governed and adhere to "slave morality" that praises the person who serves others in self-sacrifice.

33. Nietzsche: Slave morality is contrasted with the morality of the "overman" or "superman," a new kind of human being whose forerunners included Alexander the Great and Napoleon.

34. Nietzsche's thesis that there is no God, and its apparent corollary that there are no absolute and necessary criteria of right and wrong, were accepted by such twentieth-century existentialists as Albert Camus and Jean-Paul Sartre.

35. <u>James.</u> You must choose to believe or not as a live option excluding agnosticism because God's existence can neither be proved nor disproved by logic and evidence. The pragmatic choice is to believe.

36. James: If the religious beliefs are true, but there is insufficient evidence for them, then a policy of avoiding error at any cost is an irrational policy since it cuts off a person's opportunity to make friends with God.

37. Twentieth-Century Perspectives

    James's critics thought he had elevated wishful thinking to the status of proof; believers questioned his implicit assumption that God's existence cannot be established. Others said James's belief in God amounted to a gamble rather than true religious acceptance of God.

38. God and logical positivism. A central tenet of the Vienna Circle and of logical positivism is the verifiability theory of meaning, according to which the meaning of a factual proposition is the experience you would have to have to know that it is true.

39. Theological utterances such as "God exists" or "God created the world" appear unverifiable by experience, and hence meaningless.

40. The unfolding of God. **Mary Daly**, in *Beyond God the Father:* "If God is male, then the male is God."

41. Daly: Theological symbolism and communication "serve the purposes of patriarchal social arrangements."

42. Daly: Women's confrontation with the "structured evil of patriarchy" implies the liberation of all human beings, a new phase in the quest for God.

43. Daly: "God" as an intransitive verb would not be conceived as an object, implying limitation, for God as "Be-ing" (the "most active and dynamic verb of all") is contrasted only with non-being.

44. Daly: Becoming who one really is means turning one's back on "the pseudo-reality offered by patriarchy" and by that act affirming "I am"; it means facing the threat of non-being with the courage to face the anxieties of losing job, friends, social approval, and health.

45. Daly: The women's revolution must ultimately be religious; it must reach "outward and inward toward the God beyond and beneath the gods who have stolen our identity." In the absence of false gods ("God the Judge" or "God the Judge of Sin"), women are able to experience the presence of a power of being "which both is and is not yet."

Boxes

- The Black Cat
  (What the theologian finds in a dark room)

- Reductio Proofs
  (Useful for understanding the ontological argument)

- Profile: St. Thomas Aquinas

- Theology and Philosophy
  (Explanation of Aquinas's distinction)

- Profile: The Anchoress, Julian of Norwich

- Where Did You Get That Idea?
  (Comment on Descartes's view that there must be as much reality in the cause of an idea as there is "objective reality" in the idea)

- Evil
  (What the problem is, and Leibniz's solution)

- The Best of All Possible Worlds?
  (Voltaire's opinion of Leibniz's dictum)

- Miracles
  (Hume's principle for evaluating reports of miracles)

- Committee Work
  (Hume's suggestion that the world, like a camel, was assembled by committee)

- A Verbal Dispute?
  (Hume's idea that the dispute between theists and atheists is, in some ways, merely verbal)

- Creation *or* Evolution?
  (An examination of the effect on Catholicism and conservative Protestantism of the publication of Darwin's On the Origin of Species and a defense of "creation-science" from the Institute for Creation Research)

- God's Foreknowledge and Free Will
  (The difficulty involved in maintaining both)

- Religion: Illusion with a Future
  (Freud's view)

- The Consequences of Belief
  (James's pragmatism applied to the question of free will)

- Pascal's Wager
  (Either God exists or he does not; by betting that he does you lose nothing if he doesn't)

- Profile: William James

- The Big Bang
  (The Big Bang hypothesis leads to a hard choice between an unexplainable universe or one explainable only by reference to something nonphysical)

- Is This Atheism?
  (Did the logical positivists deny God's existence?)

- God Is Coming, and She Is Pissed
  (On God's gender)

- Who Needs Reasons for Believing in God?
  (Maybe God's existence, says philosopher Alvin Plantinga, is a "basic belief")

Readings

12.1 St. Anselm, from *Proslogion*

This is Anselm's first and most famous version of the ontological argument.

12.2 St. Thomas Aquinas, from *Summa Theologica*

The five ways.

12.3 Friedrich Nietzsche, from *The Gay Science*

Nietzsche's assertion that God is dead and his explanation of what it means.

12.4 Antony Flew, from "Theology and Falsification"

Flew's famous parable, developed from a John Wisdom tale, about an invisible gardener who tends a field but escapes all efforts to detect him.

12.5 Mary Daly, from *After the Death of God the Father*

A selection from *Beyond God the Father* in which Daly discusses the rootedness of theology in patriarchy, and what can be done to enable women to speak more authentically about God.

Philosophers' Principal Works

- St. Anselm (c. 1033–1109)
  Monologion
  Proslogion

- Gaunilo (eleventh century)
  In Behalf of the Fool

- Thomas Aquinas (1225–1274)
  On Being and Essence (1253)
  Truth (Quaestiones Disputatae de Veritate [1256–1259])
  Summa Contra Gentiles (1258–1260)
  On the Power of God (1265)
  Summa Theologica (1265–1269)
  In Librum de Causis (1271)

- Julian of Norwich (1342–1414?)
  Showings

- René Descartes (1596–1650)
  Discourse on Method (1637)
  Meditations on First Philosophy (1641)
  Principles of Philosophy (1644)

- Gottfried W. Leibniz (1646–1716)
  Theodicy (1710)
  Monadology (1714)
  New Essays (1765)

- David Hume (1711–1776)
  A Treatise of Human Nature (1739–1740)
  An Enquiry Concerning Human Understanding (1748)
  An Enquiry Concerning the Principles of Morals (1751)
  Dialogues Concerning Natural Religion (1779)

- Immanuel Kant (1724–1804)
  Critique of Pure Reason (1781)
  Prolegomena to Any Future Metaphysics (1783)
  Foundations of the Metaphysics of Morals (1785)
  Critique of Practical Reason (1788)
  Critique of Judgment (1790)

- William Paley (1743–1805)
  A View of the Evidence of Christianity (1794)
  Natural Theology (1802)

- John Henry Newman (1801–1890)
  - *Essay on the Development of Christian Doctrine* (1845)
  - *The Idea of a University* (1852)
  - *Apologia Pro Vita Sua* (1864)
  - *A Grammar of Assent* (1870)

- Søren Kierkegaard (1813–1855)
  - *Either/Or* (1843)
  - *Philosophical Fragments* (1844)
  - *The Concluding Unscientific Postscript* (1846)

- Friedrich Nietzsche (1849–1900)
  - *The Birth of Tragedy* (1872)
  - *Beyond Good and Evil* (1886)
  - *Twilight of the Idols* (1888)
  - *Ecce Home* (1888)
  - *Thus Spoke Zarathustra* (1883–1891)

- William James (1842–1910)
  - *Principles of Psychology* (1890)
  - *The Will to Believe and Other Essays in Popular Philosophy* (1897)
  - *The Varieties of Religious Experience* (1902)
  - *Pragmatism* (1907)
  - *A Pluralistic Universe* (1909)
  - *The Meaning of Truth* (1909)
  - *Some Problems in Philosophy* (1911)
  - *Essays in Radical Empiricism* (1912)

- Blaise Pascal (1623–1662)
  - *Pensées* (unpublished during Pascal's lifetime)
  - *De l'Esprit géométrique* (unpublished during Pascal's lifetime)

- Antony Flew (1923–)
  - *New Essays in Philosophical Theology* (ed. with Alasdair MacIntyre) (1955)
  - *The Presumption of Atheism, and Other Philosophical Essays on God, Freedom and Immortality* (1976)
  - *God: A Critical Enquiry* (2nd ed.) (1984)
  - *David Hume, Philosopher of Moral Science* (1986)

- Mary Daly (1928–)
  - *Beyond God the Father* (1973)
  - *Gyn/Ecology: The Metaethics of Radical Feminism* (1978)
  - *Pure Lust: Elemental Feminist Philosophy* (1984)

- Alvin Plantinga (1932–)
    The Nature of Necessity (1974)
    "Advice to Christian Philosophers" (1984)
    God and Other Minds (rev. ed.) (1991)
    Warrant: The Current Debate (1993)
    Warrant and Proper Function (1993)

Lecture-Discussion Ideas Related to Selected Questions

10. *Explain Hume's reasoning for remaining skeptical of reports of miracles. Is this reasoning sound?*

Hume's principle is this: before you accept a report of a miracle, stop and think. The report's being false would have to be a greater miracle than the miracle it reports, if you are to be rationally justified in accepting that report.

Hume's principle makes it difficult to accept *any* reports of miracles, and this is as it should be. On the face of things the likelihood that the person who reports having seen the miracle was deceived or deluded, or has misrecorded or misremembered what was seen, or is mentally imbalanced or is just plain lying, is greater than that the report is true. Deception, delusion, misrecording, misremembering, and mental imbalance are all common things, whereas miracles, by definition, are not. Even outright fraud, judging from the steps we take to secure ourselves against its threat, is among the most common of human activities. Turn in any direction, and you will encounter ID checks, signature verification cards, stamps, certificates, lie detectors, tests, locks, and a hundred other things whose very existence is vivid testimony that people all too commonly deceive, cheat, lie, and are otherwise dishonest.

True, Hume's principle also makes it difficult to accept strange new discoveries, findings, and theories. Back in flat-earth days it would have required many not to accept reports that the earth is round. But this, again, is exactly as it should be. Sometimes rationality requires us to reject claims that later turn out to have been true.

We would have to concede, of course, that it is not always clear when one thing is more miraculous than another. But at the very least Hume's principle helps us all remember how very strong the proof must be before we accept reports of miracles.

We want now to outline a talk that you might find useful if the topic of so-called psychic miracles ever arises in class. One of us goes out of his way to make sure that this topic does arise in his class. Far too few these days seem sufficiently critical of claims made by and for so-called psychics.

Our little talk divides itself into three parts. In the first part, having defined psychic powers (the power to possess information about the world through nonsensory means and without having inferred it from something that is present to sense), we invite the class to relate incidents that they think qualify as psychic. In the second part we discuss alternative ways of looking at coincidence. In the third part we ask the class to imagine how the world would be if people really did have psychic powers.

Here is a little more detail:

In the first part, when we ask people to tell their own psychic stories, they invariably come forth with reports of premonitions and what are called psychic crisis-coincidences. The premonition experiences usually involve dreaming about an event before it happens. The crisis-coincidences involve dreaming of a close friend or dear relative at the same time something awful happens to the person. You know the type of thing we are talking about.

The important thing is to keep track (without saying anything) of what counts as a psychic premonition or crisis-coincidence in your class. As you will probably see, what counts as psychic is not just thinking of a *close friend* or *dear relative*, for any friend or relative—or even a passing acquaintance—will do. And what counts is not just *dreaming* of the person, whoever he or she may be, for just plain thinking about him or her counts as well. And further, for a coincidence to count as psychic it is not even necessary that you think (or dream) about the person *at the time* the awful thing is happening to him or her. If the awful event happens a little before the dream (or thought), that counts. If it happens a little after, that counts too. If it even happens quite a bit before or after it may count as well. And finally, as you will see, for a coincidence to count as psychic it is not even required that what happens to the other person be *awful*. It just has to be significant in *some way or other*. The criteria for what counts as a psychic premonition have a similar looseness about them.

At the end of the first part you might suggest that what makes these various experiences seem psychic is that it seems ridiculous to suppose that they were really mere coincidences.

Everyone has now been properly primed, and it is time to move to the second part of the talk.

In this part of the talk you point out that there are two different ways of looking at coincidences. One can look at them "subjectively" or one can look at them "objectively." You look at them *subjectively* when you say, "Good grief! What are the chances that I would be thinking about my brother's son at the very time that he was falling off a cliff (or whatever)?" You look at them *objectively* when you say, "What are the chances that *someone or other* among the world's 5 billion-plus inhabitants would think *or* dream *or* daydream about *someone or other* among his friends, relatives, and other assorted acquaintances at the same time *or* a little before *or* a little after *something or other* of significance happened to him or her?" Once people start looking at these coincidences "objectively," they don't seem the least bit surprising. In fact, given how many people there are, and how many people each person knows, and how often people think or dream or daydream about someone or other they know, you would expect such coincidences to be happening to someone or other at every instant. It's like the lottery, we tell the class: the chances of *your* winning are a million to one. But the chances of *someone's* winning are dead certain. Most get the idea. In case they don't, you have to explain. "The fact that so many of you have had these experiences is not evidence of ESP, but is exactly what you would expect from coincidence. What would be really weird is if no one at all in the class had had an experience of this sort."

In the third part of the talk, we invite the class to consider what the world would be like if ESP were a common phenomenon. We ask them, for example, if there would be any point in teachers giving tests, bartenders checking IDs, police questioning suspects, bailiffs swearing in witnesses, casinos operating, or the Madame Rubies of the world reading palms for a pittance when they could make a killing on the stock market or in Vegas. No, these considerations don't show that we don't all have ESP in some vague and inchoate form, but then, what would?

16.   *Is James correct in saying that you cannot really suspend judgment about God's existence?*

James said that the agnostic backs the field against the belief in God, but many students don't quite understand what he meant. If you back the field against the favorite in a horse race, the only way you lose is if the favorite wins. If any other horse wins you get a percentage of the purse. Backing the field is a relatively safe, and somewhat timid, bet. James was implying that the agnostic tries to take the safe way out. The agnostic thinks the favorite horse, the theist's horse, won't win, but he doesn't want to risk everything on the atheist's horse, so he bets on the field. The analogy isn't exact, but it conveys a vivid image.

Theists often think of agnostics in this way, as wishy-washy atheists. For that matter, atheists too sometimes think agnostics are namby-pambies who don't have the courage to own up to atheism. So an interesting question arises. Why does agnosticism tend to be viewed by both parties as a kind of weak-kneed atheism? Why isn't it viewed as weak-kneed theism, or possibly as just plain neutral?

It must be, it seems to us, that many people agree with James that the question of God's existence is "forced"; that is, it is a question you cannot suspend judgment on. The question "Does God exist?" apparently is viewed as like the question "Are you going to shake hands with me at this very instant?"—a question to which "I don't know" as a response would be equivalent to "no."

So the question becomes, is there reason to think that "Does God exist?" is forced, and that "I don't know" is equivalent to "no"?

There is reason to think this, perhaps, if you accept the ontological argument, and believe that to understand what God is is to know that he exists. The person who accepts the ontological argument would have to maintain that anyone who says "I don't know" implies that he or she understands the question asked, and therefore understands the meaning of "God," and therefore must concede that God exists. From the point of view of an adherent of the ontological argument, if you understand what the question ("Does God exist?") means, you must either answer "yes" or fall into logical contradiction. The atheist and agnostic both, from this point of view, sleep in the same bed, because neither answer "yes."

We are tempted, therefore, to say that James's belief that the question of God's existence is forced rests on the assumption that the ontological argument is valid. Let's just keep in mind too that James's entire "proof" of God rests on his belief that that question is forced.

24.   *Assuming that there is scientific evidence that the universe had an absolute beginning, does that evidence also prove the existence of God? Explain.*

We treated this in the box (The Big Bang) in the text, but to elaborate a bit on what we said there:

Theists have maintained that the totality of natural events that is the universe requires an explanation and that that explanation must involve God. Many philosophers have said in response, agreeing with Hume, that the explanation of the totality of natural events does not require reference to God: if each natural event were explained by reference to other natural events, then the totality of events itself would have been explained without invoking God.

If, however, there were a first natural event, then that event could not be explained by reference to antecedent natural events, and the subsequent events that depended on that first event would similarly lack a purely naturalistic explanation.

So, if the theory that the universe had an absolute beginning in the Big Bang is a true theory and does entail that there was a first natural event, then we seem to face these choices:

(1) The event is unexplainable.

(2) The event is explainable, but only by reference to something supernatural.

It might be said that the first event might be given a naturalistic explanation that does not require mentioning earlier events or conditions. But what kind of explanation would this be?

Option (1), it might be noted, is difficult to accept psychologically only because every event that we have experienced has been caused. But let's not forget that the first event, if it was not caused by God (and maybe even if it was) happened *ex nihilo*. Now, we don't have any experience of something's coming to exist *ex nihilo*. And because we do not have any such experience, it is an unwarranted extension of our experience to maintain that what is true of events that we have experienced must also be true of such events as something's coming to exist *ex nihilo*. We don't have experience of anything even remotely like the first natural event, so we cannot apply the lessons of experience to it. Once this fact is realized, it seems to be a lot less difficult to suppose that the first event (if there were such a thing) really did just happen, without explanation.

25.   *Is the belief that the proposition "'God exists' is meaningless" a form of atheism?*

Some theists will probably so regard it, but this seems to be a mistake, since "God does not exist" is presumably equally meaningless.

It is worth noting too that the belief likewise is not a form of agnosticism. The agnostic doesn't know whether or not God exists; he or she therefore finds the question "Does God exist?" intelligible but as yet unanswered. Suspicious students can be brought around by asking them a question in a language they don't understand. Their answer will be "What?" After translating the question, you ask them if their answer (which meant, in effect, "Your question is meaningless to me") was a form of agnosticism.

Another question that might be asked is where an individual who doesn't know whether or not "God exists" is meaningless stands relative to the original issue of whether God does exist. (Don't ask this question if you wish to maintain the idea that philosophy works with explosive and dangerous material.) The answer to this question seems to be that if you don't know whether or not it is meaningless to say that God exists, then you can be neither an atheist nor a theist nor an agnostic, because agnosticism, atheism, and theism all assume that "Does God exist?" is not meaningless. If your position is that you don't know whether or not it is meaningless to say that God exists, you are agnostic, but not as to whether God exists but as to whether atheism, theism, or religious agnosticism are tenable positions. The question is sheerly an exercise.

CHAPTER 13

An Era of Suspicion

Main Points

1. Diverse Continental philosophers have been suspicious about Western metaphysical systems they claim lead to the manipulation of nature or set up a certain cultural perspective as absolute truth.

2. <u>Jürgen Habermas</u>

   Habermas: "Positivistic science" defines the "objective" experimental method as the criterion of truth. When its methods are applied to human beings people are treated as objects; but what is needed is a method that would treat human beings as the subjects they are. Such a science Habermas called historical/hermeneutic because it explores the "practical" interest each of us has in understanding others.

3. Hermeneutics deals with principles of interpretation.

4. Aside from being unable to produce "practical understanding" of our intersubjective worlds, positivistic science is also inadequate in providing what Habermas calls "emancipatory knowledge." This is the concern of critical theory: making explicit the controlling ideology of a political or social order.

5. For Habermas, knowledge of the ideologies that shape our communication can be liberating as we reflect on the most deeply held assumptions of our society. Truly nonideological, rational communication is the "ideal speech situation" presupposed, Habermas says, in every discourse.

6. Michel Foucault

    Foucault, in his "archaeological" period, claimed to have found a series of discontinuous "created realities" or "epistemes" that serve each historical era as the ground of what is true and what is false. Yet because the charting of the various epistemes seemed itself to assume a kind of objectivity on the part of the researcher, Foucault abandoned archaeology in favor of genealogy.

7. For Foucault (taking up the work Nietzsche had earlier begun), genealogy committed the observer to no universal theory of reality; the emphasis in genealogy was not knowledge, but power. In his later work Foucault traced the development of various forms of power manipulation within society as he examined prisons, insane asylums, and hospitals. He found each institution perpetuating its work in part by redefining its mission. Though doctors no longer see themselves as casting out evil spirits, surgeons (by redefining disease) have maintained the "priesthood" of the medical profession.

8. Structuralism Versus Deconstruction

    Structuralism is a methodology that seeks to find the underlying rules and conventions governing large social systems such as language or cultural mythology.

9. **Saussure**: Linguistics is the study of signs, defined as a combination of the signifier (the physical thing that signifies) and the signified (that which is signified). The meaning of signs in a sentence depends not only on the order of the signs but on the contrast of each sign with other signs in the language that are not present.

10. **Lévi-Strauss** adapted Saussure's methods and applied them to ethnographic research to find the underlying structures of thought in the myths of nonindustrial societies.

11. The analysis of sign systems of various types, from advertising slogans to animal communication, is called semiotics.

12. **Derrida** broke with French structuralism (which was concerned with the "deep structures" of language common to all speakers) by announcing that no definitive meaning of a text could ever be established. Derrida's "deconstructive" method showed what he called the "free play of signifiers."

13. Derrida is suspicious of any claim to final interpretation

14. Richard Rorty

    Rorty is suspicious of the traditional claims of philosophy itself to have the methods best suited to finding "truth." "There is no method for knowing when one has reached the truth, or when one is closer than before."

15. Rorty's pragmatic definition of truth: whatever "survives all objections within one's culture." Standards are relative to one's culture and such starting points (standards of evidence, reasonableness, knowledge) are contingent.

16. For Rorty, "what matters is our loyalty to other human beings clinging together against the dark, not our hope of getting things right."

17. <u>Feminist Critiques</u>

    <u>Sexism and language.</u> The use of "man" to express the concept of humanity as well as the male gender tends to obscure the role of women in society; slang terms for women tend to reflect certain hostile dispositions to them (an older unmarried man is a "swinging single" or "happy bachelor" but an older unmarried woman is an "old maid").

18. **Stephanie Ross** argues that metaphors associated with women (such as "screw" in describing sexual intercourse) reflect demeaning cultural attitudes toward women.

19. <u>Pornography.</u> Pornography tends to objectify women and according to some researchers tends also to equate sex and violence (specifically violence against women). Feminist thought differs over whether pornography plays a significant role (causal or otherwise) in the incidence of rape and other forms of violence against women.

20. <u>The importance of recognizing diversity.</u> Most women who have dominated feminist thinking have been white and middle-class; women from different racial and/or class backgrounds have felt excluded from the development of feminist theory. An important question for women of color is whether sexism or racism is the more fundamental social problem.

21. <u>Feminist epistemology.</u> Feminist thought has challenged mainstream epistemology (which assumes the ideal knower is disembodied, purely rational, fully informed, and completely objective). Feminist epistemologists point out that even supposedly objective scientists import their own prejudices and biases into their observations.

22. Knowledge-gathering is a human project and reason, but also emotion, social class, gender, and other factors play a role in what is "known." Any ideal that rules out the "human factor" in its characterization of knowledge will unjustly privilege the group claiming that true knowledge is only obtainable by people who are just like them and have only their social characteristics.

23. <u>Ecofeminism.</u> **Val Plumwood**: The "inferiorization" of both women and nature are linked; both are grounded in the rationalist conception of human nature and the liberal-individualist conception of the human self.

24. Plumwood: The "rationalist framework" is among other things a network of value dualisms (mind/body, reason/emotion, masculine/feminine) that defines the first/superior item in opposition to the second/inferior item, with the interests of the first/superior item taking priority over those of the second/inferior item.

25. Plumwood: In the mind/body dualism, "nature is divided off, is alien, and usually hostile and inferior."

26. Plumwood: The liberal-individualistic conception of the self portrays the self as autonomous and as lacking essential connections to other individuals. Nature is viewed as a resource, and so are other people.

27. Plumwood: The "relational view of self," which views humans as social beings with interdependent interests, is more accurate than the purely disconnected and egoistic view of the self; further, it recognizes that nature is distinct from self but at the same time affirms the human continuity with nature.

28. Plumwood criticizes the environmental philosophies of **Paul Taylor** and **Tom Regan** for being embedded in the rationalist framework. Taylor emphasizes the reason/emotion dualism in calling for environmental ethics based on principles, and Regan's concept of rights becomes absurd when applied to natural ecosystems.

29. What is needed is a richer moral stance that reevaluates reason/emotion and other dualistic contrasts, attaches importance to ethical concepts concerning emotionality and special relationships, and abandons the exclusive focus on the universal and the abstract.

Boxes

- Frankfurt School
  (*Habermas and Herbert Marcuse are associated with this school*)

- Philosophical Anthropology
  (*What is a human being? The answer may not be all that clear*)

- Profile: Michel Foucault

- Pornography and the Law
  (*The work of Catharine MacKinnon and Andrea Dworkin*)

- Backlash
  (*Susan Faludi's 1991 indictment of journalistic ethics, especially in the reporting of studies relating to women's health and happiness*)

Readings

13.1   Michel Foucault, from *The History of Sexuality*

Is modern bourgeois society sexually repressed? No, according to Foucault, as he here explains.

13.2   Michel Foucault, from *Madness and Civilization*

Is modern civilization conducive to insanity?

13.3   Karen J. Warren, from "The Power and the Promise of Ecological Feminism"

On the nature of a feminist ethic and "how ecofeminism provides the framework for a distinctively feminist and environmental ethic."

Philosophers' Principal Works

- Jürgen Habermas (1929–)
  Knowledge and Human Interests (1971)
  Theory and Practice (1973)
  Legitimation Crisis (1975)
  Communication and the Evolution of Society (1979)
  Observations on the Spiritual Situation of the Age: Contemporary German Perspectives (1984)
  On the Logic of the Social Sciences (1988)
  The New Conservatism: Cultural Criticism and the Historians' Debate (1989)
  Moral Consciousness and Communicative Action (1990)
  The Past As Future (1994)

- Michel Foucault (1926–1984)
  Madness and Civilization: A History of Insanity in the Age of Reason (1965)
  The Order of Things: An Archaeology of the Human Sciences (1970)
  The Birth of the Clinic: An Archaeology of Medical Perception (1973)
  Discipline and Punish: The Birth of the Prison (1977)
  The History of Sexuality, Volume I: An Introduction (1978)
  The Use of Pleasure (Vol. II of The History of Sexuality) (1985)
  The Care of the Self (Vol. III of The History of Sexuality) (1986)

- Ferdinand de Saussure (1857–1913)
  Course in General Linguistics (1916)

- Claude Lévi-Strauss (1908–)
  Structural Anthropology (1963)
  The Savage Mind (1966)
  The Jealous Potter (1988)

- Jacques Derrida (1930–)
  Of Grammatology (1976)
  Writing and Difference (1978)
  Of Spirit: Heidegger and the Question (1989)
  Acts of Literature (1992)
  Memoirs of the Blind: The Self-Portrait and Other Ruins (1993)
  Specters of Marx: The State of the Debt, the Work of Mourning, and the New International (1994)
  The Gift of Death (1995)
  On the Name (1995)

- Richard Rorty (1931–)
  Philosophy and the Mirror of Nature (1979)
  Consequences of Pragmatism (1982)
  Contingency, Irony, and Solidarity (1989)
  Objectivity, Relativism, and Truth (1991)
  Essays on Heidegger and Others (1991)
  Achieving Our Country (1998)
  Truth and Progress (1998)

- Stephanie Ross (1949–)
  "How Words Hurt: Attitude, Metaphor, and Oppression" (1981)

- Val Plumwood
  "Nature, Self, and Gender: Feminism, Environmental Philosophy, and the Critique of Rationalism" (1991)

- Tom Regan (1938–)
  "The Nature and Possibility of an Environmental Ethic" (1982)
  The Case for Animal Rights (1983)
  The Thee Generation: Reflections on the Coming Revolution (1991)

- Andrea Dworkin
  Women Hating: A Radical Look at Sexuality (1976)
  Right-Wing Women: The Politics of Domesticated Females (1983)
  Intercourse (1988)
  Pornography: Men Possessing Women (1989)

- Catharine MacKinnon
  Feminism Unmodified: Discourse on Life and Law (1987)
  Toward a Feminist Theory of the State (1989)
  Only Words (1993)

Lecture-Discussion Ideas Related to Selected Questions

9. *How are the feminist criticisms of pornography different from the more fundamentalist, right-wing criticisms of pornography on TV or in the papers?*

Students will often remark on the similarities between right-wing and left-wing analyses of social problems. In many respects, they are quite correct; right-wing and left-wing political thinkers do tend to provide very similar fundamental explanations of social problems. They both differ from liberals, who tend to analyze all social problems from the point of view of methodological individualism. In contrast, right- and left-wing thinkers analyze social phenomena from the perspective of methodological holism, leading to an initial appearance of similarity.

The differences between right- and left-wing thinkers become glaring when we turn to the solutions they offer. Feminists and fundamentalists both think that pornography is degrading to women and that it manifests certain hostile, antisocial values. Right-wing fundamentalists, however, wish to turn back to rigidly structured social patterns in which women are respected, in a sense, but are restricted to the roles of wife and mother. Feminists, on the other hand, wish to move forward and discard the earlier, more constrained social organizations. They reject the idea that women should be put on a pedestal; instead, they argue for greater equality and freedom. Both right-wingers and feminists find pornography antithetical to an ideal social order, but their ideals are sharply at odds with each other.

CHAPTER 14

Eastern Influences

Main Points

1. <u>Hinduism</u>

   Hinduism is the Western term for religious beliefs and practices (with an associated philosophy) of the Indian people, going back into the unknown past.

2. The basis of Hindu philosophy is the belief that reality is absolutely one, that there is only one ultimate reality-being-consciousness. The belief-system ranges from belief in primitive deities to sophisticated metaphysical theories.

3. Common to all forms of Hinduism is acceptance of the Vedic scriptures. Philosophically, the most important Vedic scripture is the last book, the Upanishads, best known for the theories of brahman (ultimate cosmic principle of reality) and atman (the inner self) and the identification of brahman and atman.

4. There are four great sayings of the Upanishads; all are ways of saying that brahman and atman are one: (1) Consciousness is brahman; (2) that art thou; (3) the self is brahman; (4) I am brahman. The identification of brahman and atman has been subject to various interpretations (several of which are explained in the text).

5. Much of the wisdom of Hinduism lies in its sages, including, in the twentieth century, Rabindranath Tagore, Aurobindo Ghose, and Mohandas K. Gandhi.

6. <u>Buddhism</u>

   Buddhism, which arose in India, was originally a response to the problem of suffering. Suffering is in part the result of the transience and uncertainty of the world, in part the result of karma, and in part the result of ignorance and enslavement by desires and passions.

7. Buddha. Buddha's answer to this problem is contained in the Four Noble Truths and the Eightfold Path. Through meditation and self-abnegation, promotion to better lives and finally to nirvana is obtained.

8. Additional concepts attributed to Buddha: clinging to existence must be overcome; and silence of body, mind, and speech must be achieved.

9. Taoism

    Three great systems of thought dominate Chinese civilization: Taoism, Confucianism, and Buddhism.

10. Taoism derives from Lao Tzu and Chuang Tzu.

11. Lao Tzu. Regarded Confucian attempts to improve society by direct action as hopeless. Lao Tzu thought (as later did Socrates) that the wisest are still very ignorant. What is needed is not interference with the world but humble understanding of the way it functions, the Tao. Forcing change is self-injurious. Follow the Tao instead, the natural order of things. The Tao gives rise to yang and yin, and is the means by which things come to be, take shape, and reach fulfillment. The Tao cannot be improved.

12. The sage cultivates tranquillity and equilibrium so as to recognize the Tao. He is selfless, cares for all things, and seeks to benefit them rather than to use them for his own ends. He is modest, slow, and cautious, and in some respects like water in behavior and results.

13. Enduring change is brought about by weakness, not by strength; by submission, not by intervention. In the political sphere, the use of force brings hostility and retaliation. The wise ruler sidesteps problems by anticipating them. He is nonacquisitive and does not seek to impose his way of thinking on others.

14. Chuang Tzu. The most important Taoist next to Lao Tzu, Chuang Tzu held that nature (the world) has its own wisdom and cannot be forced or hurried in its unfolding in the Tao. Because the Tao and not the person determines what will happen, the wise person accepts the course of events as it unfolds, with neither hope nor regret.

15. The sage ruler remains free from selfish desires, anticipates crises before they arise, and is always tranquil. Opposites are in fact equal as a single entity within the Tao. The sage does not distinguish himself from the Tao.

16. Chuang Tzu emphasized the danger of usefulness. The sage avoids becoming too useful.

17. <u>Confucianism</u>

   Confucian political philosophy has dominated Chinese life in a way unequalled by the thought of any similar philosopher in the West.

18. <u>Confucius.</u> Set forth ideals of behavior based on his understanding of the Way, the path taken by natural events (not a fixed and eternal transcendental principle). Humans are perfectible. The Way works through the principle of the Mean, and human behavior should avoid extremes and seek moderation.

19. Confucius's principle of reciprocity: "Do not do to others what you would not want them to do to you."

20. The sage represents, in effect, an ethical ideal. Sageship requires knowledge of change and the order of things, including correct understanding of human relationships and the workings of nature. It also includes correct use or rectification of names. The sage's conduct is superior because he patterns his behavior on the great of the past, and because he learns from personal experience. His fairness makes the sage trusted by rulers and all.

21. The roots of ignoble governance are greed, aggressiveness, pride, and resentment. The viciousness of the ruler infects the governed. The ruler governed by the Mean rules justly and impartially, seeks equal distribution of wealth, promotes security and peace, and rules virtuously by example and not by force of arms.

22. The family too should be patriarchal and authoritarian, and its proper functioning depends on the obedience of the subordinate members and on its responsible governance in accordance with the Mean.

23. The five primary human relationships: between ruler and subject, parent and child, elder and younger brother, husband and wife, and one friend and another.

24. <u>Mencius.</u> Like Confucius, Mencius (the second greatest Confucian philosopher) believed that people are potentially good and was optimistic as to human betterment through conscientious conduct. He believed the way to the upright life, and true happiness, must include difficulty, suffering, and toil; helping one's family and society; and leadership.

25. Disorder in a state is often caused by the indifferent and selfish ruler. The state governed without vision falls into ruin and death. Killing the monarch of the disordered state is not murder. The good ruler exhibits benevolence, righteousness, and propriety, and is knowledgeable.

26. <u>Zen Buddhism.</u> Buddhism came to China and mixed with Taoism, Confucianism, and other influences to become Chinese Zen Buddhism.

27. <u>Hui Neng.</u> The story of Hui Neng's investiture as the Sixth Patriarch of Chinese Zen.

28. The ultimate Dharma: Hui Neng gave it several titles: the Self-Nature; the Buddha-Dharma; the Real Nature; the eternal and unchanging Tao.

29. There are no "things"—all things are one. Human thought imposes thirty-six basic pairs of opposites (such as light and darkness; yin and yang; birth and death; good and bad, and so on) in order to make sense of a totality that cannot be grasped at once. This ultimate reality is an absolute state of suchness or reality or truth that neither goes nor comes, increases nor decreases, is born nor dies.

30. Freedom from selfish, one-sided visions of reality is accomplished through a state of no-thought or mindlessness.

31. Stirring up the melting pot of Eastern philosophy. By the late ninth century Japanese culture reflected an unequal mixture of Shinto, Confucianism, Taoism, and Zen Buddhism (and its Mahayana branch, with the two further branches of Tendai and Shigon.

32. Shinto, an ancient native religion of Japan, related humans to the kami, or gods of nature, that created the universe. This animist view regarded people as "thinking reeds" completely a part of the natural and divine universe.

33. People's duties were derived through their blood relationships. Connection to the gods of nature came through the ancestor's clan and through the divine clan of the Mikado who was both national high priest and head of state.

34. Mahayana Buddhism incorporated the Confucian virtues of filial piety, veneration of ancestors, duties based on rank and position, honesty, and the like. Mahayana saw humanity unified through spiritual enlightenment in the worship of one god—the Mikado, the greatest earthly kami. This was the form of Buddhism adopted by Japanese aristocracy.

35. Murasaki. Murasaki Shikibu: Shinto Buddhist feminist philosopher who rejected mainstream Buddhism's view of women, which believed them to be of lesser moral worth than men. Women could achieve salvation, or reach the psychological state of nirvana that would prepare them to enter the Western Paradise, but only after reincarnation as a male.

36. Murasaki represents a minority Buddhist view that women are moral agents who, instead of blaming fate, can assume moral responsibility for their actions. She held that women should challenge their karma (destiny) and take control of their own lives. The long process of philosophical enlightenment can begin, not after reincarnation as a male, but rather in the present life, living according to the teachings of Shinto Buddhism.

37. Dogen. Founded the Soto branch of Japanese Zen Buddhism.

38. Dogen: Life is impermanent; therefore do not waste it. Time must be utilized in a worthy pursuit, in an all-out effort for a single objective. Yet the rapidity of life makes it difficult to decide how best to manage oneself. The mind overwhelmed by a world not understood seeks safety in selfish and self-protective acts. The perception of the world as good and bad, right and wrong, black and white, is the "Lesser Vehicle," and arises out of ignorance and fear.

39. Dogen: The solution is to practice the Great Way, to see things from the perspective of the universe or Buddha Dharma or universal Self: the wisdom of emptiness. This requires seeking to help others without reward or praise. (Thus Dogen endeavored to set forth a way to achieve permanent joy in this life.)

40. The Philosophy of the Samurai (c. 1100–1900)

   The wisdom of the samurai was transmitted through the centuries in the form of martial precepts that were used to teach the art of bushido (the art of being a samurai warrior); the literature of the samurai has influenced all areas of Japanese thought and behavior.

41. The brevity and uncertainty of life requires preparedness and anticipation: "Win beforehand." That other people are flawed in character requires self-reliance.

42. The complete man is both scholar and warrior. He understands the importance of the Confucian principle of the Mean. He is humane, wise, courageous, polite, dignified, proper in dress and speech, and absolutely truthful.

43. Members of the samurai class went to Zen monks for training to achieve a state of fearlessness. Fear arises through excessive attachment to self, which can be overcome only through constant meditation on death.

44. The influence of Confucius. The model of the perfect samurai closely follows the Confucian idea of the complete man.

45. The influence of Zen Buddhism. The Zen and samurai traditions both emphasized attainment of an unobstructed state of instant, untainted response: mushin, the state of no-mind and no-thought.

46. Islamic Philosophy (see box)

47. Neoplatonism and Aristotle played an important role in shaping Islamic philosophy, which arose in the eighth century during Western Europe's Middle Ages.

48. Avicenna envisioned God as a Necessary Being who emanated the contingent, temporal world out of himself.

49. Averroës taught the idea of eternal creation; some interpreted Averroës as teaching the doctrine of double truth: a separate truth of philosophy and a separate truth of religion.

50. Sufism represents a mystical and ascetic strain of Muslim belief that seeks union with God (Allah).

51. Sufism was influenced by the mystical tendencies of Neoplatonism and gnosticism. Through ascetic practices and concentrated inwardness, a human being might experience a sudden illumination and a sense of ecstatic union with God (Allah).

Boxes

- Ommmmm
  (What "ommmmm" is)

- Profile: Siddhartha Gautama Buddha

- Buddhism and the West
  (The parallel concerns of the Buddhists and Stoics; the influence of Buddhist thought on Schopenhauer; contemporary influences)

- Eastern Philosophy and Eastern Religion
  (They are intertwined)

- Islamic Philosophy
  (A short survey)

- Lao Tzu
  (Quotations)

- The Tao, Logos, and God
  (A brief comparison of these three concepts)

- Lao Tzu on Virtuous Activity
  (Quotations)

- Lao Tzu and the Martial Arts
  (Extensions of Taoist philosophy to the martial arts)

- Lao Tzu on Government
  (Quotations)

- Chuang Tzu
  (Quotations)

- Cook Ting
  (Chuang Tzu's famous story)

- Chuang Tzu on Virtuous Activity
  (Quotations)

- Profile: Confucius

- Confucius's Humanism
  ("The measure of man," he said, "is man")

- Confucius: Insights on Life
  (Quotations)

- Confucius on Government
  (Quotations)

- Confucius's Worldliness
  (It is with this world that Confucius was concerned)

- Mencius
  (Quotations)

- Mencius on Virtuous Activity
  (Quotations)

- Mencius and Thomas Hobbes on Human Nature
  (The two compared and contrasted)

- Mencius on Government
  (Quotations)

- Hsün Tzu
  (Unlike Mencius, he believed human beings to be basically bad)

- Zen and Ch'an
  (Both words come from the Sanskrit word for meditation)

- Hui Neng's Poem of Enlightenment
  (Ultimate reality is beyond all conceptualization)

- Hui Neng
  (Quotations)

- Profile: Murasaki Shikibu

- Zen Buddhism in Japan
  (About the two major traditions)

- Dogen's Prescriptions for Virtuous Activity
  (Quotations)

- The Ancient Philosophies Today
  (A few brief words on the subject)

- Courage and Poetry
  (The importance of poetry to the warrior)

- The Magnificent Seven
  (Concerning the John Sturges version of Akira Kurosawa's film classic, The Seven Samurai*)*

- Governance by the Warrior
  (Why the warrior class replaced the court aristocracy)

- Samurai Insights (from Yamomoto Tsunetomo, *The Hagakure*)
  (Quotations)

Readings

14.1   Confucius, from *Analects*

Book I of the sayings of Confucius.

14.2   Dwight Goddard, ed., from *The Buddhist Bible*

A traditional elaboration of the Noble Eightfold Path.

Philosophers' Principal Works

- Al-Kindi (d. after A.D. 870)
  On First Philosophy

- Al-Farabi (c. A.D. 872–950)
  On the Perfect State
  Commentary and Short Treatise on Aristotle's De Interpretatione

- Avicenna (A.D. 980–1037)
  The Book of Healing
  Canon of Medicine

- Al-Ghazali (A.D. 1058–1111)
  Incoherence of the Philosophers

- Averroës (A.D. 1126–1198)
  The Incoherence of the Incoherence
  Decisive Treatise on the Agreement between Religious Law and Philosophy

- Lao Tzu (seventh or sixth century B.C.)
  Tao Te Ching

- Chuang Tzu (fourth century B.C.)
  The Complete Works

- Sun Tzu (sixth century B.C.)
  The Art of War

- Confucius (551–479 B.C.)
  The Analects

- Mencius (371–289 B.C.)
  The Book of Mencius

- Hui Neng (A.D. 638–713)
  The Sutra of Hui Neng

- Murasaki Shikibu (A.D. 970–1031)
  Tale of Genji

- Dogen Zenji (A.D. 1200–1253)
  A Primer of Soto Zen
  Records of Things Heard

- Miyamoto Musashi (A.D. 1584–1645)
  A Book of Five Rings

- Yamamoto Tsunetomo (A.D. 1659–1719)
  The Hagakure
  The Book of the Samurai

- Yagyu Munenori (A.D. 1571–1646)
  "Heiko noSho"
  Kinsei Geido Ron

- Basho (A.D. 1644–1694)
  The Four Seasons
  Back Roads to Far Towns
  A Haiku Journey
  The Way of Silence

Lecture-Discussion Ideas Related to Selected Questions

1.   *Do you believe in reincarnation? Why, or why not?*

Gallup and other polls indicate that a sizable percentage of Americans believe in reincarnation, and our own informal surveys of our classes support this. If you care to lecture on the subject from a Western, analytical, skeptical point of view, here are a few of our thoughts on the subject.

The theory of reincarnation is one of four main theories of life after the death of the existing body. The other theories are those of resurrection, disembodied survival, and astral-body survival.

Hume, we seem to recall, thought that reincarnation was the only theory of life after death that made any sense.

It's not a bad idea to mention that these all are theories of *personal* survival, survival of one*self*. Some students want to talk about living on as part of a cosmic consciousness or as a series of vibrations or energy waves or the like (though these notions seem less popular now than they did some years ago), but if you point out that such theories don't promise survival of the self, they (the theories) lose their attractiveness.

A popular theoretical objection to reincarnation assumes memory as essential to personal identity: I am John Locke only if I remember having had some of John Locke's experiences. When we speak of this as a popular objection, we mean only that it is popular among philosophers. It will not even have occurred to your students, rest assured.

Getting a class to appreciate this objection can take much of a class period. One approach we have used is to make up very short biographies of two individuals whose lives do not overlap temporally. We then ask why what we have read counts as two biographies and not as one; that is, why it doesn't count as a case of reincarnation. "Why, nothing ties the two people together," the class will point out. We then tie the two biographies together by adding one additional sentence to the biography of the later person, a sentence to the effect that he or she remembers having had some of the former person's experiences. Voilà!—a case of reincarnation, thanks to addition.

Of course, all you have shown is that remembering an earlier person's experiences is a sufficient condition of being that person, not that it is a necessary condition. You therefore must ask the class if they can think of any way other than through memory to tie the two biographies together. Someone may try to make the connection by having the two individuals share the selfsame soul. If someone tries this, you are in for a full day if you don't remember that all you want to do is to show that the memory objection is plausible.

You don't want to try to show more than that, either. That's because the memory objection to reincarnation does not really *prove* that you are not, or were not, some past person, John Locke or whoever. After all, even though you don't *now* remember any of Locke's experiences, you might in the future, or in a future life, or under hypnosis. However, you can still say that, as long as you lack memories of Locke's experiences, it is a matter of no consequence whether or not you are Locke.

Other objections to reincarnation are (1) it doesn't account for expansions and contractions of the human population; (2) the explanation of a person's properties, both psychological and physiological, as due to heredity and environment, is much more plausible than any alternative that postulates reincarnation; and (3) empirical evidence of reincarnation is wanting.

Objections (2) and (3) are the best objections and are really quite powerful. Of course they are not the kind of iron-clad, knock-out disproofs that philosophers like. Further, (3) will be questioned by believers, if any you have, who have their own supply of anecdotes suggestive of reincarnation, "Bridey Murphy" type stories.

Such anecdotes are almost always subject to simpler explanations that don't involve assumption of prior lives.

Introducing Eastern philosophy through poetry.

Literature, especially poetry, offers a wonderful approach to Oriental philosophy. Chinese poetry, for example, movingly presents experiences that correspond to those of even young, career-directed college students: the longing for love, the joy of friendship, the uncertainty and unfairness of fate, the melancholy of lost happiness, and the constraints of duty. Chinese poems help make even the more abstract maxims of Taoism, Buddhism, and Confucianism seem concrete and meaningful.

The most appealing poetry to Western ears, maybe, is that of Po Chü-i (772–846), who was a government official during the Tang period. Po Chü-i wrote several thousand poems noted for their simple and graceful elegance. To read them is to experience his gratitude and appreciation for life and the beauty of nature. Arthur Waley is noted for his exquisite rendering of the subtlety and refinement of Po Chü-i and other Chinese poets. This poetry will help your students understand the modest recommendations of Chinese philosophers.

Japanese literature also provides an excellent introduction to Japanese philosophy. You might wish to consider, for example, some of the collections of popular proverbs and sayings from Zen masters, such as are contained in *A Zen Forest*, translated by Soiku Shigematsu and published by Weatherhill. Also available are collections of stories and lessons that disclose some of the insights of Zen and Japanese thought generally: you might consult Paul Reps's *Zen Flesh, Zen Bones* (Rutland, Vermont: Charles E. Tuttle). Other backup works worth looking at are Joe Hyams's *Zen in the Martial Arts* (Bantam Books in New York) and Michael Minick's *The Wisdom of Kung Fu* (originally from William Morrow and Co., Inc., New York).

One of the best books for the samurai tradition is *Ideals of the Samurai: Writings of Japanese Warriors*, published by Ohara Publications, Inc., of Burbank, California.

Finally, R. H. Blyth wrote a series of small books in which he attempted to reveal the wisdom of Zen by illustrating it through relevant Oriental and Western poems. A version of these writings was published by E. P. Dutton & Co., Inc., in 1960, and entitled *Zen in English Literature and Oriental Classics*.

CHAPTER 15

Other Voices

Main Points

1. Post-colonial thinkers, such as Mahatma Gandhi, Martin Luther King Jr., Fidel Castro, Malcolm X, and Desmond Tutu, do their work in recollection of deep cultural traumas that have occurred in the histories of their respective peoples.

2. Post-colonial thought takes up problems of cultural dissolution and questioning previously unquestioned worldviews. It challenges an uncritical acceptance of the notion of progress.

3. Direct appeals for justice are not sufficiently compelling to bring about change; thus, raising consciousness through philosophy has become an important undertaking.

4. A principled perspectivism has become an accepted part of post-colonial writing; in the twentieth century, some form of Marxism has been the overwhelming theoretical choice among Third World writers.

5. Among the topics most intensively developed in post-colonial studies of history and justice has been the matter of domination.

6. Historical Background

   Models of colonization: in the fifteenth century, the Iberian powers (Spain and Portugal) extracted valuable metals and other commodities from the areas under their control for shipment back to the mother country; British colonies in the eighteenth century were developed to be markets for manufactured goods; in Southeast Asia the French instituted a colonial model midway between the Spanish and British systems.

7. Whatever the model, colonization entailed (a) violent physical subjugation of indigenous peoples and (b) the introduction of the colonizers' values and beliefs into traditional societies.

8. Post-colonial thought tries in various ways to come to terms with a history of subjugation and revolutionary impulses; in the colonial and former colonial powers post-colonial thought has been marginalized or dismissed altogether, though among subjugated and formerly subjugated populations post-colonialist thinkers have become social and political leaders (Mahatma Gandhi in India, Kwame Nkrumah in Ghana, Léopold Senghor in Senegal, Ho Chi Minh in Vietnam, Vaclav Havel in the Czech Republic).

9. The shared experience of domination has helped to structure a general revolutionary consciousness among subjugated peoples of the Third World.

10. Though post-colonial thinkers frequently disagree with others from within their own traditions about interpretations of events and situations, post-colonial thought is distinctive in self-consciously dealing with the dislocations brought on by encounters with conquerors whose imperialism aimed at near-total domination.

11. Thus, the commonalties of post-colonial thought are not so much derived from the conceptual similarities among local traditions, as from similarities among experiences of invasion and foreign domination.

12. Africa:

    Pan-African philosophy is a cultural categorization of philosophical activity that includes the work of African thinkers and thinkers of African descent wherever they are located.

13. After centuries of contact between African and non-African cultures, it is difficult to isolate a set of purely traditional African philosophical positions; but Africanists point out that thinkers have always appropriated and reworked the ideas of others (so, for example, it is likely Egyptian concepts play a part in the thinking of such European figures as Pythagoras and Plato). The drawing of intellectual boundary lines that tended to exclude African thought has become suspect.

14. The most promising question to guide an inquiry into Pan-African philosophy is not what a purely African philosophy is, but how philosophy has been done in Africa and in the places outside Africa where Africans have resettled, whether voluntarily or by force.

15. Oral and traditional philosophy. *Person*: What a person is is a metaphysical question; that is, it is more an invention of human beings than an inherent fact of nature, and thus the idea of person varies from culture to culture.

16. *The nature of philosophy*: **Paulin Hountondji** focuses on the task of deconstructing texts that, in his analysis, perpetuate a colonial mentality. He has been most concerned with two problem influences: ethnophilosophy and the advocacy of the concept of negritude.

17. He argues that practitioners of ethnophilosophy (which seeks to describe traditional beliefs) impose external categorizations on those they study but justify their work in terms of its usefulness to those who would control African consciousness by manipulation of symbols and concepts.

18. The same problem, says Hountondji, afflicts the adherents of the negritude position, which in effect valorizes the African soul at the expense of the African intellect, and ironically perpetuates colonialist thought.

19. *Historiography*: **Léopold Sédar Senghor** outlined a distinctive African epistemology to explain the claim that there was an African way of knowing that was different from the European. His doctrine of negritude, widely misunderstood, arose from his phenomenological method and claimed that African cultures evaluate metaphors differently from European ones.

20. *The good life*: Over time, the consciousness of people brutalized by colonial regulations, which tend to benefit only a few, may become distorted and traditional values may fall into obscurity. Countering the tendency requires vigilance and discipline; some recommend socialism, some democracy, some religion. All recommend justice.

21. Archbishop **Desmond Tutu** is one of the architects of South Africa's revolutionary transition from apartheid to representative democracy; his opposition to economic exploitation and official brutality has been heard around the world.

22. <u>The Americas</u>

    Native Americans from the Toltecs to the Onondagas engaged in vigorous campaigns of empire-building, but with the coming of the Europeans, imperial ambitions in the Americas were pursued from a position of technological superiority that the colonized native peoples could not match and with a sustained, single-minded acquisitiveness outside the experience of most tribes.

23. With first-person accounts of genocidal aggression still part of the experience of many Native Americans, the post-colonial philosophical response has only begun to enter the literature.

24. African-American post-colonial thinking occurs not only in self-identified philosophical texts, but also in story and song; for most post-colonial thinkers, allowing the possibility of departures from the stylistic norms of philosophy is a strength—any occasion may open up a space for philosophical reflection.

25. The introduction of Marxism to Latin America, which occurred mostly outside the traditional academic circles, provided the first serious challenge to the hegemony of Roman Catholic metaphysics. By the middle of the twentieth century, a major part of Latin American philosophical discourse had taken on a heavily religious cast.

26. Except where Marxist materialism has been consciously adopted, religiously metaphysical claims regularly serve as points of departure or elements of the presuppositional structures of post-colonial texts. In their own terms, this does not make them any less philosophical; rather, it is a way of engaging the whole person in the act of thinking and interpretation.

27. <u>African-American thought.</u> *Social justice*: **Martin Luther King, Jr.**, was strongly influenced by the example and the writings of Mahatma Gandhi in seeking a world where his children "one day soon . . . will no longer be judged by the color of their skin but by the content of their character."

28. *Sexuality*: In the African-American community, awareness of the successes of the civil rights movement and the rise of feminism in the white middle class combined with firsthand knowledge of a mostly unwritten history of the particular difficulties of black women, including a high incidence of domestic violence, to produce a variant of feminism that is especially sensitive to the social-ethical questions of marginalization. Middle-class feminism, **bell hooks** argues, was liable to be co-opted by the existing power structure to perpetuate a culture of competition and individualism.

29. *Afrocentrism*: **Chaikh Anta Diop**, an Africanist, argued that among other things black Africa was the origin of Egyptian civilization and that Europeans who were not purely Nordic traced their ancestry back to Africa. The matter is still very controversial.

30. **Molefi Kete Asante**: Afrocentrism's chief architect.

31. *Nihilism*: By definition, seeing all things and possibilities as worthless and dead. Nietzsche revived the issue for Western philosophy; in his analysis, nihilism in European society arose out of a refusal to abandon caution and grasp one's own destiny, wherever it might lead. In the modern world, nihilism is not just an affliction of Europeans.

32. Nihilism, as well as issues of social activism, are addressed by **Cornel West**, Professor of Afro-American Studies and the Philosophy of Religion at Harvard University.

33. <u>Latin American thought.</u> One feature that distinguishes Latin American thought from most European philosophy is the sustained effort to explore the relevance of philosophy to problems of social justice.

34. *Ontology*: The branch of philosophy that concerns itself with the question of being.

35. Recent writings of Latin American philosophers demonstrate the possibility of interpreting the work of Heidegger and Sartre in ontology in new ways. For example, Argentinian philosopher **Carlos Astrada** takes Heidegger's thinking as evidence of the collapse of the bourgeois mentality that determined much of the course of colonial activity, especially in the perpetuation of unequal distributions of wealth inherited from colonial times.

36. Recent history and the pace of technological change plant doubt about the stability of existence, so it is no surprise that a school of philosophy, existentialism, should arise that sees the fundamental fact of existence as one of becoming.

37. For post-colonialist thinkers, it is not surprising that the wealthy would project the instability of their own power structures onto the existence of humanity itself; Astrada shows that works of existentialist ontology can be read as political-economic texts.

38. *Metaphysics of the human.* No claims of philosophic foundationalism have stood the tests of time; but the moral and metaphysical claims of the ruling elites (past and present) demand constant vigilance and persistent critique. Marx called these foundational claims ideology (a kind of self-interested delusion that infected the bourgeoisie and was half-consciously passed on to the proletariat).

39. Though Marx believed the proletariat would eventually realize that the ideological claims of the bourgeoisie were without merit and that such ideology could be contradicted, Peruvian philosopher **Francisco Miró Quesada**, however, suggests that contradicting the claims of one group with the claims of an alternative theory of reality creates conflict and thus suffering. Instead, humanity itself must be reimagined.

40. Quesada: (a) Theories cannot reliably deliver the truth and (b) much suffering is caused when people take theories too seriously. He proposes to divide the human race into those who are willing to exploit people and those who are willing to defend them from exploitation.

41. *Gender issues.* Mainstream feminism, as a movement of middle-class European and American women, appears not to speak well to the conditions of marginalized peoples. Two major expansions of feminism have been suggested by voices outside the mainstream: (a) Feminism ought to pay more attention to issues of class and (b) abandon a black-white racial dichotomy (which excludes the majority of women in the world who are neither). **Sonia Saldívar-Hull** insists that her "white feminist 'sisters' recognize their blind spots" in the use of the black woman to signify "all dispossessed women."

42. <u>South Asia</u>

    According to a majority of contemporary analysts, colonialism has been economically and socially destructive in the former South Asian colonies, such as Vietnam, Cambodia, and Laos. Some analysts claim the colonialist introduction of modern political infrastructure and value systems have helped former colonies succeed in a technologically sophisticated world.

43. Unlike the cultures of sub-Saharan Africa, the nations of Asia have traditions of written philosophy stretching back longer than in the West by at least a thousand years.

44. The shock of colonialism to Asia was deep, but not so comprehensive for these cultures that their philosophers have felt impelled to the kind of sustained reflection and cultural reconstruction that has been prominent in Africa. Instead, outside ideas and techniques, from British aesthetics to Marxist political-historiographical philosophy, were appropriated and reworked to conform to indigenous values.

45. India endured two centuries of economic despoilment at the hands of the mercantilist-capitalist forces of Britain. Ironically, the introduction of British values into India created the conceptual resources that Indians would use to remake their society (after expelling the British).

46. Asian writers often couch their discussions in terms of the abstract principles and linear inferences typical of Western philosophy, though this stylistic similarity is not a borrowing from Western thought but a continuation of local traditions of discourse.

47. <u>Satyagraha.</u> The concept, closely identified by the social and political thinking of **Mohandas (Mahatma) Gandhi**, means "clinging to truth" or the force of what is inadequately translated as "passive resistance."

48. For traditional Indian philosophy, the discipline needed in the search for truth was not simply a matter of acquiring the tools of scientific investigation; one also had to practice such virtues as giving, nonattachment, and noninjury in order to develop mental purity. Gandhi is a part of this tradition in his adoption of its rigorous demands for personal integrity and cultivation.

49. But Gandhi was also a student of Thoreau and Tolstoy; he repudiated the claims of human inequality by circumstances of birth that underlay the caste system.

50. <u>Metaphysics.</u> Once other cultures entered the Indian sphere of consciousness, they were evaluated to see not only how they met the standards of indigenous tradition but also how they might be recast to fit into the Hindu framework.

51. For **Rabindranath Tagore**, who developed his sense of a possible modern Indian consciousness in poetry and essays, such a consciousness can come only if the true nature of human beings is acknowledged and actions carried out accordingly. Indian tradition provides a guide to the complexities of human nature and the behaviors needed for a harmonious and enlightening life. This understanding is developed throughout one's life, so human beings must devote themselves to living the examined life.

Boxes

- Oral Philosophy
  (If it's not written, can it be philosophical?)

- Colonialism and the Church
  (An ambiguous legacy)

- Profile: Desmond Tutu

- Profile: Martin Luther King Jr.

- Black Power
  (A look at the influential 1960s movement in the United States)

- Profile: bell hooks (Gloria Watkins)

- Profile: Cornel West

- Liberation Theology
  (Christian social activism in Latin America, with philosophical roots in Continental philosophy)

- Profile: Mohandas Gandhi

- Profile: Rabindranath Tagore

Readings

15.1   Léopold Sédar Senghor, from *On African Socialism*

An African "way of knowing" that is different from the European.

15.2   Desmond Tutu, from "My Vision for South Africa"

On the nature of the good life.

....

Philosophers' Principal Works

- Léopold Sédar Senghor (1906–)
  The Mission of the Poet (1966)
  The Collected Poetry (1991)

- Desmond Tutu (1931–)
  Hope and Suffering: Sermons and Speeches (1983)
  Crying in the Wilderness: The Struggle for Justice in South Africa (1986)
  The Nobel Peace Prize Lecture (1986)
  The Rainbow People of God: The Making of a Peaceful Revolution (1994)

- Martin Luther King, Jr. (1929–1968)
  The Trumpet of Conscience (1987)
  The Measure of a Man (1988)
  I Have a Dream: Writings and Speeches That Changed the World (1992)
  Letter From the Birmingham Jail (1994)

- bell hooks (c. 1955–)
  Talking Back: Thinking Feminist, Thinking Black (1989)
  Yearning: Race, Gender, and Cultural Politics (1990)
  Black Looks: Race and Representation (1992)
  Outlaw Culture: Resisting Representations (1994)
  Teaching To Transgress: Education as the Practice of Freedom (1994)
  Killing Rage: Ending Racism (1995)

- Chaikh Anta Diop
  The African Origin of Civilization (1974)

- Molefi Kete Asante (1942–)
  The Afrocentric Idea (1987)
  Afrocentricity (1988)
  Kemet, Afrocentricity, and Knowledge (1990)
  Malcolm X as Cultural Hero: And Other Afrocentric Essays (1993)

- Cornel West (1953–)
  The American Evasion of Philosophy: A Genealogy of Pragmatism (1989)
  The Ethical Dimensions of Marxist Thought (1991)
  Beyond Eurocentrism and Multiculturalism (1993)
  Keeping Faith: Philosophy and Race in America (1993)
  Race Matters (1993)

- Carlos Astrada (1894–1970)
  Existentialism and the Crisis of Philosophy (1963)

- Mohandas (Mahatma) Gandhi (1869–1948)
  The Moral and Political Writings of Mahatma Gandhi (1986–1987)
  An Autobiography: The Story of My Experiments With Truth (1993)

- Rabindranath Tagore (1861–1941)
  The Religion of Man (1988)
  The English Writings of Rabindranath Tagore (1994–)

Lecture-Discussion Ideas Related to Selected Questions

General note about questions for chapter 15:

The issues raised here are intended to transcend provincial boundaries. The answer that any particular individual might give to these questions, however, will be tied to a concrete cultural/historical situation, and thus will vary from one instance to another. This is not to say that all possible answers are equal, but one should allow conceptual space for a variety of well-motivated answers. In evaluating student essays, the instructor will want to keep in mind the diverse *styles* of philosophy modeled in the chapter. If the instructor plans to prefer some styles of discourse over others in student writing, the preferences should be made clear to students.

1. *Is a person only a body? Can you think of two alternative understandings of what is essential to a person?*

Richard C. Onwuanibe argues in "The Human Person and Immortality in Ibo (African) Metaphysics" that the materialist conception of the person is not the only plausible understanding. Specifically, he takes issue with the notion that the person should be totally identified with the body. In doing so, he accepts a burden of proof that requires him to go against the view that the only meaningful evidence for a factual claim is that which comes to us through the sort of investigation conducted in the experiments of the natural sciences. Onwuanibe knows that he cannot restrict himself to materialistic assumptions and criteria in his attempt to refute the materialist position, for that would amount to capitulation before he had even begun to state his case.

In contrast to the materialist view that "I am totally this body," Onwuanibe proposes the traditional Ibo conception of the person as a complex of body and soul. He vigorously denies the reasonableness of reducing human beings to pure physicality. He observes phenomenologically that people in virtually every culture speak in ways that indicate a sense of self that transcends the physical body. Instead of saying, "I am totally this body," they will say, "I have this body" or "I have a body." At stake in this issue is not just the factual matter of whether or not the materialist conception of the human being is adequate, but the coherence of our understanding of human experience generally.

The key to Onwuanibe's argument is the fact of subjective transcendence revealed in the sense of the presence of other persons. First, there is the realization that persons are somehow more than just their physical facticity or the social roles they play. Second, there is the undeniable option of relating to others either as other subjects or as objects; the mere fact that the choice exists means that human beings are capable of recognizing personhood as such. Here, Onwuanibe's phenomenological investigation of consciousness demonstrates not only that there is support for his claim that there exists a reasonable alternative to the materialist/physicalist view of the person, but also that one need not rely on materialist methodology to assemble meaningful evidence for this alternative.

It is important to note, claims Onwuanibe, that the personhood he describes cannot be reduced to more primitive components. Though one might wish for the relative simplicity of the fundamental entities of most scientific and technological operations, this is not possible when trying to understand persons. There can be no compromise on the issue of the integrity of the person in Ibo metaphysics. That the person is an irreducible subjective reality may require acknowledging something mysterious and not readily discoverable about existence, but given the evidence of our own experience, this alternative is still better than the false clarity of reductive materialism.

10. *What does Senghor mean by the phrase "sympathetic reason"?*

When Senghor advocates sympathetic reason, he is not just talking about a way of thinking, but a way of being in the world. Sympathetic reason, in Senghor's definition, refers to a complex process of acquiring understanding that he says is typical of black Africans.

Moreover, he asserts that if one develops a good understanding of sympathetic reason, one will be able to explain important differences between black African cultures and European cultures. That there are differences is undeniable; Senghor wants to explain these differences in a way that satisfies not only the person creating the explanation, but also all parties referred to by the explanation. He is well aware that Africans and Europeans have diverse ideas about his theory, and that racial characteristics seem to play little part in determining who accepts his claims and who rejects them. Actually, that fact might be taken as weak evidence against the claims he is making, but that would be a hard argument to make.

Essentially, sympathetic reason entails bringing oneself into virtual identity with the thing one wants to know. In this state of identification of self and other, all the senses and capabilities to discover are brought into play. In the operation of sympathetic reason, separateness dissolves in an experience of creative discovery. This, says Senghor, is not pure emotion. It must be understood as a definite kind of reason, one that he says is closer to the Greek concept of *logos* than the Latin concept of *ratio*. In making this contrast, Senghor not only has in mind the larger scope of meaning of *logos*, but also the history of the concept's role in the thinking of being. Sympathetic reason, because of its more holistic epistemology, enables the knower to appreciate the being of the other in ways that the more abstract *ratio* inhibits.

This energetic way of knowing, which does not hold things at arm's length to get "objective distance" on a problem or question, is a superior choice, claims Senghor. In his understanding, Europe's reason of the eye gives way to the reason of the embrace. Clearly, Senghor cannot mean sympathetic reason is superior for every purpose, especially if one honestly includes developing technology, conquering territory, and a host of other things people have considered important throughout history. Instead, a reasonable reading of Senghor suggests that this path of participation excels at helping the individual develop a deep understanding that includes a large element of appreciation. Senghor, in effect, is seeking to redefine how we understand thinking in order to encompass new possibilities.

For post-colonial thinkers, the critical possibilities that have presented themselves through the redefinition of terms and reconstruction of contexts have been extremely important. In this case, Senghor shows that it is possible to reconceptualize epistemology in a way that makes traditional European rational methods look limiting and unnecessarily oblivious to the body. If it is accepted that Africans have been using a more comprehensive mode of thinking, Senghor will have succeeded in bringing the world to accept a new basis for interpreting the achievements of African civilizations. That, in turn, furthers the post-colonial project of retrieving native cultures from the coercions of conquerors' histories and categorizations.

SECTION II

OBJECTIVE QUESTIONS

CHAPTER 1

Powerful Ideas

True/False

1. The word *philosophy* comes from two Greek words that mean "keeper of the flame."
    F

2. For ancient Greek thinkers, philosophy included subject matter that today would be called physics and psychology.
    T

3. *Normative* questions ask about the value of something, such as what ought to be valued as good or beautiful.
    T

4. It is generally accepted today that philosophy has proven that human beings have free will.
    F

5. Logic is a branch of philosophy.
    T

6. Epistemology is concerned with the nature and possibility of knowledge.
    T

7. Metaphysics studies the nature of knowledge.
   F

8. Epistemology and aesthetics both consider the same basic questions.
   F

9. In philosophy, as the text points out, one person's opinion is as valid as the next person's opinion.
   F

10. According to the text, it is a mistake to think that truth is personal.
    T

11. An argument is created when someone supports a belief by giving a reason for accepting that belief.
    T

12. Ad hominem arguments, appeals to emotion, and straw man arguments might all be said to be red herrings.
    T

13. Consider the following: "The reason I know abortion is wrong is because I know murder is wrong." This argument is an example of begging the question.
    T

14. Another name for the "black-or-white fallacy" is "begging the question."
    F

Multiple Choice

15. Which of the following is *not* a historical subdivision of philosophy?
    A.* Prehistoric philosophy
    B. Ancient philosophy
    C. Medieval philosophy
    D. Modern philosophy
    E. Contemporary philosophy

16. Which of the following would *not* be included in the tradition of Continental philosophy?
    A. Existentialism
    B.* Analytic philosophy
    C. Phenomenology
    D. Hermeneutics
    E. Critical Theory

17. Consider the following argument: *"Whatever is caused had to occur, given the exact state of the world at the time.* If a choice is voluntary, it did not have to occur, given the state of the world at the time. Therefore, voluntary choices cannot be caused." The sentence in italics is called a
    A.   Fallacy
    B.*   Premise
    C.   Conclusion

18. "Your argument that there's too much violence on television doesn't hold water. Why, just look at the great kids' shows—there's Mr. Rogers's Neighborhood, Sesame Street, the New Captain Kangaroo. Those shows are great!"
    A.   Begging the question fallacy
    B.   Black-or-white fallacy
    C.*   Red herring fallacy
    D.   No fallacy; good argument

19. "The views philosopher Martin Heidegger has about modern technology have to be rejected. After all, the man supported the Nazis!"
    A.   Straw man fallacy
    B.*   Argumentum ad hominem fallacy
    C.   Begging the question fallacy
    D.   No fallacy; good argument

CHAPTER 2

Early Philosophy

True/False

1. The first metaphysician was Thales.
   T

2. Metaphysics is the study of the occult.
   F

3. According to Theano, Pythogoras said that all things are numbers.
   F

4. Heraclitus maintained that all change was fundamentally random.
   F

5. Parmenides based his philosophy on systematic observation.
   F

6. The concept that observable changes in the universe are in reality changes in basic particles was first suggested by Empedocles.
   T

7. Mind or reason, according to Anaxagoras, created matter.
   F

8. The Atomists said the universe was composed of infinitely divisible particles.
   F

9. Democritus is likely to have made a "Persian-to-Persian" call.
   T

10. The Atomists were determinists.
     T

Multiple Choice

11. Which of the following is the "fundamental metaphysical question"?
     A.   How should I live?
     B.   What can I know?
     C.* What is the nature of being?
     D.   What is the perfect form of government?

12. Which philosopher is *not* considered a pre-Socratic?
     A.   Anaximenes
     B.   Anaxagoras
     C.   Leucippus
     D.* Aristotle

13. Which doctrine characterized the thinking of Parmenides?
     A.   Empirical investigation
     B.* A priori reasoning
     C.   Being is ceaselessly changing
     D.   Being has many parts

14. Which is *not* true of Empedocles?
     A.   He proclaimed himself a god
     B.   He said the forces that caused change were Love and Strife
     C.   He was a competent scientist
     D.* He said the basic building blocks of the universe were atoms

15. The Atomists believed that the motion of atoms
     A.   Fulfilled the gods' purposes
     B.* Was governed by physical laws
     C.   Was only apparent, not real
     D.   Proved there was no such thing as empty space

16. Which philosopher was a Milesian?
     A.* Thales
     B.   Pythagoras
     C.   Aristotle
     D.   Zeno of Elea

17. Which philosopher attempted to demonstrate that motion was impossible?
     A.   Thales
     B.   Pythagoras
     C.   Aristotle
     D.* Zeno of Elea

18. Which philosopher said that permanence is an illusion?
    A.   Parmenides
    B.* Heraclitus
    C.   Anaximenes
    D.   None of the above

19. Anaxagoras
    A.   Introduced philosophy to Athens
    B.   Introduced the distinction between matter and mind
    C.   Believed *nous* was the source of all motion
    D.* All of the above

CHAPTER 3

Socrates, Plato, and Aristotle

True/False

1. Xenophanes said that even if truth were known, it could not be stated.
   F

2. Cratylus said communication is impossible because the words we speak change in meaning even as we speak them.
   T

3. The Sophists of ancient Greece were skilled debaters and speechwriters who would try to devise an argument to support any claim and who taught others to do the same, all for free.
   F

4. The Sophist Protagoras affirmed that "man is the measure of all things."
   T

5. In his dialogues, Plato said that knowledge may be equated with sense perception.
   F

6. The Form of "circularity" or "beauty" can only be grasped intellectually, according to Plato.
   T

7. Some of Plato's Forms were of a higher order than others.
   T

8. Plato believed that changes in an object's underlying Form account for our perception of change.
   F

9. The "Third Man argument" was used in support of Plato's Theory of Forms.
   F

10. Aristotle maintained that every physical object was a combination of matter and form.
    T

11. Aristotle explained change in terms of movement from potentiality to actuality.
    T

12. In Aristotle's view, universals such as "humanness" or "dogness" exist independently of particular humans or dogs.
    F

Multiple Choice

13. Which of the following is *not* true of Socrates?
    A. An oracle had called him the wisest of men
    B.* He wrote a number of dialogues
    C. He was convicted by the Athenians for religious heresy
    D. His philosophical approach involved a search for proper definitions

14. Which of the following characterizes a Platonic Form?
    A.* It is eternal
    B. It is always in motion
    C. It exists in the physical world
    D. It is in the realm of sensible things

15. Which does *not* apply to Plato's metaphysics?
    A. Two realms
    B. Theory of Ideas
    C. Indivisible Forms
    D.* No independent existence apart from particular objects

16. Plato is famous for his allegory of the
    A. Rock
    B. Coin
    C.* Cave
    D. Blocks

17. Which of the following is *not* true of Aristotle?
    A.* Plato studied under Aristotle at the Academy
    B. Aristotle tutored Alexander the Great
    C. Aristotle was a "peripatetic"
    D. Aristotle disagreed with Plato's doctrine of Forms

18. For Aristotle, the "efficient cause" of something meant
    A. What the thing is
    B. What the thing is made of
    C.* What made the thing
    D. What purpose the thing serves

19. Which philosopher said that Forms are universals?
    A. Plato
    B.* Aristotle
    C. Leucippus
    D. Aristocles

CHAPTER 4

The Philosophers of the Hellenistic and Christian Eras

True/False

1. Plotinus was a Neoplatonist philosopher.
   T

2. Plotinus's god, like the Christian God, was a personal deity.
   F

3. Plotinus would have been pleased if you threw a birthday party for him.
   F

4. Neither Plato nor Plotinus were Christians.
   T

5. Both St. Augustine and Plato maintained a "two realms" concept of reality.
   T

6. Hypatia was sympathetic to the metaphysics of Plotinus.
   T

7. Hypatia died peacefully, surrounded by her friends and family.
   F

8. Hypatia rejected mathematical proofs as having nothing to do with philosophy.
   F

9. Sextus Empiricus, the greatest skeptic of ancient times, was a Pyrrhonist.
   T

10. *Ataraxia* means tranquillity.
    T

11. A total skeptic is one who suspends judgment in all matters or maintains that
    nothing can be known.
    T

12. The Pyrrhonists and the Academics both proclaimed that nothing can be known.
    F

13. Pyrrho's fame was apparently primarily a result of his exemplary *agoge.*
    T

14. St. Augustine said that skepticism was refuted in the very act of doubting.
    T

15. The theory that universals exist outside the mind is known as realism.
    T

16. For both Aquinas and Aristotle, explanations in terms of ends or goals were to be
    rejected.
    F

Multiple Choice

17. Plotinus's "god" would *not* be described as
    A.   Utter transcendent
    B.*   The Creator
    C.   Indescribable
    D.   The One

18. Of what was St. Augustine speaking when he said "If no one asks of me, I know; if I
    wish to explain to him who asks, I know not"?
    A.   God
    B.   Eternity
    C.*   Time
    D.   Creation

19. Which doctrine of St. Augustine was at odds with Neoplatonism?
    A.   The unchanging God
    B.*   The Incarnation of Jesus Christ
    C.   The nature of evil
    D.   The timelessness of God

20. Hypatia wrote an important commentary on
    A.*   Ptolemy
    B.   Aristotle
    C.   Descartes
    D.   Copernicus

21. Who tried to refute the claim that there is no absolute knowledge?
    A.   Gorgias
    B.   Protagoras
    C.   Pyrrho
    D.*   None of the above

22. Which of the following is true of St. Augustine?
    A.   He was the first "Christian skeptic"
    B.*   He said the law of noncontradiction refuted skepticism
    C.   He revived the Academic school
    D.   He said there was no knowledge in sense perception

23. Which of the following is *not* a characteristic of a modified skeptic?
    A.*   Such a skeptic doubts that anything is actually known
    B.   Such a skeptic denies or suspends judgment on the possibility of knowledge
          from, say, history or metaphysics
    C.   Such a skeptic denies or suspends judgment on the possibility of knowledge
          from, say, reason or experience
    D.   Such a skeptic denies or suspends judgment on the possibility of knowledge
          of God

24. Which of the following is *not* true of Aquinas's metaphysics?
    A.   It blended Christianity with the philosophy of Aristotle
    B.   *What* something is is not the same as *that* it is
    C.*   God's existence can only be known by faith
    D.   God is the pure act of existence

25. Who is most likely to have written this? "But if the senses do not apprehend
    external objects, neither can the mind apprehend them; hence, . . . we shall be
    driven, it seems, to suspend judgment regarding the external underlying objects."
    A.   Augustine
    B.   Aquinas
    C.   Plato
    D.*   Sextus Empiricus

26. *Epoche* means
    A.   A causal explanation
    B.*   Suspension of judgment
    C.   Tranquillity
    D.   A kind of egg

CHAPTER 5

The Modern Period

True/False

1. Metaphysical materialism, idealism, and physicalism are dualistic philosophies.
   F

2. According to the text, today's "commonsense" metaphysics rejects the old "two worlds" view of Plato.
   F

3. In the early part of the seventeenth century, Pierre Gassendi and Marin Mersenne argued against skeptics who claimed the true nature of things was unknowable.
   F

4. Modern philosophy began with René Descartes.
   T

5. Descartes's motive in using the methods of the skeptics was to destroy any possibility of certain knowledge whatsoever.
   F

6. Using his methodology of doubt, Descartes affirmed that his belief in a God who would not deceive him was beyond doubt.
   T

7. Descartes appealed to the "clear and distinct criterion" of certainty.
   T

8. Descartes provided an answer to how immaterial mind can influence material substance that even today has not been successfully challenged.
   F

9. René Descartes, Benedictus de Spinoza, and Baron Gottfried Wilhelm von Leibniz were collectively known as the Continental rationalists.
T

10. John Locke, George Berkeley, and David Hume were collectively known as the British empiricists.
T

11. Thomas Hobbes hobnobbed with Galileo.
T

12. Hobbes subscribed to a kind of dualistic metaphysics.
F

13. Perception, according to Hobbes, occurs when motion outside us causes "phantasms."
T

14. According to the text, metaphysical materialism would seem to deny that an immaterial God exists, that humans have free will, and that there is life after death.
T

15. Anne Conway believed that all things are reducible to a single substance that is itself irreducible.
T

16. According to Conway, all created substances are either mental or physical.
F

17. Conway held that God, even though he is changeless, existed *within* the dimension of time.
F

18. Benedictus de Spinoza was a pantheist.
T

19. History records that Spinoza died when he fell into his lens-grinding apparatus and made a spectacle of himself.
F

20. The most difficult question for Spinoza's metaphysics was how to explain the interaction of mind and body.
F

21. In Spinoza's system, human free will is an illusion.
T

22. John Locke said that at birth, the human mind is essentially a "blank slate."
    T

23. "Representative realism" is the theory that we perceive objects indirectly by means of our "representations" of them.
    T

24. George Berkeley denied that matter existed.
    T

25. George Berkeley maintained that representative realism provided good reasons for affirming the existence of sensible objects.
    F

26. Berkeley said the perceiving mind of God made possible the continued existence of sensible things when no other mind is perceiving them.
    T

27. The empiricist is, in effect, a type of modified skeptic.
    T

28. All rationalists would argue against the theory of innate ideas.
    F

Multiple Choice

29. The view that "only the mental exists" is
    A.   Materialism
    B.* Idealism
    C.   Dualism
    D.   Neutralism

30. The time period of the Enlightenment or Age of Reason is
    A.   The fourteenth through sixteenth centuries
    B.   The seventeenth century
    C.* The eighteenth century
    D.   The late nineteenth to early twentieth centuries

31. According to Descartes, which of the following is *inaccurate*?
    A.* The essential attribute of material substance is weight
    B.   The essential attribute of mind is thought
    C.   Matter and mind are totally independent of each other
    D.   Matter and mind interact with each other

32. Which of the following is *not* associated with Descartes?
    A.* *Tabula rasa*
    B. *Cogito, ergo sum*
    C. Dream conjecture
    D. The "clear and distinct" test

33. "Parallelism" is a kind of explanation designed to apply to which theory?
    A. Materialism
    B. Idealism
    C.* Dualism
    D. Double aspect theory

34. Who is most likely to have written this? ". . . for the existence of an idea consists in being perceived. . . . Extension, figure, and motion are only ideas existing in the mind. . . ."
    A. René Descartes
    B. Anne Conway
    C.* George Berkeley
    D. Thomas Hobbes

35. Who is most likely to have written this? "I am, I exist, is necessarily true each time that I pronounce it, or that I mentally conceive it."
    A.* René Descartes
    B. Anne Conway
    C. George Berkeley
    D. Thomas Hobbes

36. Who is most likely to have written this? "All which qualities, called sensible, are in the object that causes them but so many several motions of the matter, by which it presses our organs diversely."
    A. René Descartes
    B. Anne Conway
    C. Benedictus de Spinoza
    D.* Thomas Hobbes

37. Who is most likely to have written this? "But the Eternity of Creatures is nothing else but an Infinity of Times, in which they ever were, and ever will be without end. Neither is this Infiniteness of Times equal to the Infiniteness of God's Eternity because the Eternity of God himself hath no Times in it."
    A. Thomas Hobbes
    B. Émile du Châtelet
    C. Benedictus de Spinoza
    D.* Anne Conway

38. Who is most likely to have written this? "[T]here is a great difference between mind and body, inasmuch as body is by nature always divisible, and the mind is entirely indivisible."
    A.* René Descartes
    B. Thomas Hobbes
    C. Anne Conway
    D. Benedictus de Spinoza

39. According to Spinoza,
    A. Thought and extension are attributes of two separate kinds of substances
    B.* Thought and extension are attributes of one basic substance
    C. God is the personal Judaeo-Christian God
    D. The living person is a composite of two different things, one finite and one infinite

40. Hobbes and Spinoza would agree that
    A. What exists is both material and mental, depending on how it is conceptualized
    B. What exists is only material
    C. What exists is only mental
    D.* What exists is only one substance

41. Both Descartes and Berkeley
    A. Were clergy
    B. Were monists
    C.* Took the "epistemological detour"
    D. Thought the concept of "matter" was inherently contradictory

42. Which of the following does *not* apply to Émile du Châtelet?
    A. She was a Newtonian
    B. Believed in action at a distance
    C.* She was a Cartesian
    D. She was Voltaire's lover

43. Which of the following did Berkeley *not* argue for?
    A. Size, shape, and color are perceived qualities
    B. Perceived qualities are only ideas
    C. Ideas exist only in the mind
    D.* There is no difference between "unreal" dream objects and "real" objects (since both are "in the mind")

44. The doctrine that "there's nothing in the intellect that wasn't first in the senses" was accepted by
    A. The rationalists
    B. Plato
    C.* The empiricists
    D. Descartes

45. Who subscribed to this belief? Since we do not ourselves cause our ideas of tables or chairs and other sensible things, we must reason that some other will or spirit does—God.
   A.   Descartes
   B.* Berkeley
   C.   Conway
   D.   Locke

46. Who is most closely associated with the phrase "*esse est percipi*"?
   A.   Descartes
   B.* Berkeley
   C.   Conway
   D.   Locke

CHAPTER 6

The Eighteenth and Nineteenth Centuries

True/False

1. The epistemology of David Hume is a development of the thesis that all our ideas come from experience.
   T

2. Hume maintained that we have a direct knowledge of the self or mind (described as an unchanging immaterial substance within us).
   F

3. Hume said experience reveals no necessary connection between a cause and an effect.
   T

4. Hume believed that inferences about what the future would be like, based as they were on present and past events, were justified by experience itself.
   F

5. Immanuel Kant argued that it is possible for us to have knowledge of external objects as they are in themselves.
   F

6. Immanuel Kant believed that some knowledge, at least, could be certain.
   T

7. Kant disagreed with David Hume's position that all knowledge begins with experience.
   F

8. Kant maintained that perceptions by themselves are "blind."
   T

9. According to Kant, the mind imposes a certain form and order on experienceable objects.
   T

10. Kant argued that we understand cause and effect in part because we remember the "constant conjunction" of certain repeated events.
    F

11. In the first part of the nineteenth century, the German Absolute Idealists said that reality is the expression of *infinite* or *absolute* thought or reason.
    T

12. Johann Gottlieb Fichte, Friedrich Wilhelm Joseph von Schelling, and Georg Wilhelm Friedrich Hegel were all Absolute Idealists.
    T

13. Georg Wilhelm Friedrich Hegel said that what is most real—the Absolute—is thought thinking of itself.
    T

14. For Hegel, the actual structure of thought was dualistic.
    F

15. For Hegel, "Spirit" is the synthesis of "Idea" and "Self-conscious thought."
    F

16. Hegel was nicknamed "the old man."
    T

17. John Stuart Mill distinguished between what is directly given to us in perception and what we know on the basis of inference.
    T

18. For Mill, a table is a "permanent possibility of sensation."
    T

Multiple Choice

19. David Hume said that
    A. All our knowledge is limited to what we experience and what we discover by reason
    B. All our knowledge is limited to what we discover by reason
    C.* All our knowledge is limited to what we experience
    D. Infinite knowledge is possible (in principle)

20. Who is most likely to have written this? "... Reason is the *substance* of the Universe; viz., that by which and in which all reality has its being and subsistence. On the other hand, it is the *Infinite Energy* of the Universe. ..."
    A.   David Hume
    B.   Immanuel Kant
    C.   John Stuart Mill
    D.* G. W. F. Hegel

21. Which of the following is *not* one of Hume's (main) assumptions?
    A.   Thought, knowledge, belief, conception, and judgment each consist of having ideas
    B.   All ideas are derived from, and are copies of, impressions of sense or inner feelings
    C.* No claim that something exists is a factual claim
    D.   Factual claims can be established only by observation or by causal inference from what is observed

22. Who is most likely to have written this? "The mind is a kind of theatre, where several perceptions successively make their appearance; pass, re-pass, glide away, and mingle in an infinite variety of postures and situations. ..."
    A.   Immanuel Kant
    B.* David Hume
    C.   G. W. F. Hegel
    D.   John Stuart Mill

23. According to Kant
    A.* The mind imposes spatiotemporal relations on the things we experience
    B.   We can have knowledge of things-in-themselves
    C.   What we can't know doesn't exist
    D.   Human reason can never discover categories and principles that apply absolutely and without exception to experienceable objects

24. Who is most likely to have written this? "Time is therefore a purely subjective condition of our (human) intuition ... and in itself, apart from the subject, is nothing. ... Time is the formal *a priori* condition of all appearances whatsoever."
    A.   G. W. F. Hegel
    B.   John Stuart Mill
    C.   David Hume
    D.* Immanuel Kant

25. Which of the following claims would be *rejected* by Kant?
    A.* All knowledge arises from experience
    B.   Relative to the experienceable world, Kant was not a skeptic
    C.   Relative to *das Ding-an-sich*, Kant was a skeptic
    D.   Perceptions, to qualify as experience, must be connected together or unified in one consciousness

26. Kant said that objects outside the mind must conform to that which the mind imposes on them in experiencing them. If this theory is correct, which would also be the case?
    A.   We have absolute knowledge of things-in-themselves
    B.* David Hume was wrong
    C.   We can be absolutely certain that we will never encounter dirt that is lighter than air
    D.   Our experience gives rise to an understanding of space and time

27. Which of the following is *not* true of Hegel's metaphysics?
    A.   It maintained that the individual mind is the vehicle of infinite thought reflecting on itself
    B.   It maintained that the Absolute is "becoming"
    C.   It said that Reality is a kind of integrated whole
    D.* It said that the triadic structure of the Absolute is a *method* by means of which we discover truth

28. Which of the following is *not* true about John Stuart Mill?
    A.   He was an empiricist
    B.* He was an Absolute Idealist
    C.   He was British
    D.   He was a nineteenth-century philosopher

29. The distinction between phenomena and noumena is most closely associated with
    A.   G. W. F. Hegel
    B.* Immanuel Kant
    C.   John Stuart Mill
    D.   David Hume

CHAPTER 7

The Continental Tradition

True/False

1. Existentialism, phenomenology, and analytic philosophy together are known as "Continental philosophy."
   F

2. According to Søren Kierkegaard, "sickness-unto-death" is the central philosophical problem.
   T

3. According to Arthur Schopenhauer, human beings are blindly driven by their wills in pursuit of selfish desires.
   T

4. Friedrich Nietzsche sought in his writings to reform Christianity so that it could provide the foundation for a new European civilization.
   F

5. According to Nietzsche's *Thus Spoke Zarathustra*, the "most despicable man" is called the "last man."
   T

6. Playwright Eugène Ionesco is associated with the tradition known as Dadaism.
   F

7. For existentialist Albert Camus, the principal philosophical question was how to rebuild the intellectual foundation of a civilization wracked by war.
   F

8. Camus believed that life as we find it is absurd.
   T

9. For Camus, suicide was the only valid alternative to the tragedy of life.
F

10. Existentialist Jean-Paul Sartre maintained that human beings are radically free to discover the objective values that exist in the universe.
F

11. For Sartre, the person who pretends he or she is not free shows inauthenticity and bad faith.
T

12. Sartre was not an analytic philosopher.
T

13. Sartre maintained that God did not exist.
T

14. Throughout his life, Sartre refused to advocate partisan political causes.
F

15. Both Sartre and Immanuel Kant stressed the universalization of moral choices, though for different reasons.
T

16. Sartre maintained that only through acceptance of our responsibility may we live in authenticity.
T

17. Sartre's dictum that "existence precedes essence" meant human morality could in principle be objectively grounded.
F

18. Edmund Husserl agreed with Sartre that the crisis of European civilization was in large part due to a misplaced faith in rational abstraction and idealistic metaphysics.
F

19. The scientific dualistic distinction between appearance and reality formed the basis of Husserl's transcendental phenomenology.
F

20. Husserl called for a "return to the things [i.e., phenomena] themselves."
T

21. According to Martin Heidegger, Being itself has been forgotten.
T

22. Heidegger said most human beings live unthinking lives because they suffer from "everydayness."
    T

23. For Heidegger, the innermost nature of the human being is fundamentally selfish.
    F

24. Heidegger said that thought cannot impose itself on Being because Being makes thought possible.
    T

25. According to Heidegger, the best poetry can enable human beings to find the enlightenment they need—which they can find only within themselves.
    F

Multiple Choice

26. Kierkegaard's emphasis on the utter irrationality of the world was in opposition to the belief of
    A.   Heidegger
    B.   Husserl
    C.* Hegel
    D.   Hölderlin

27. Which is *not* a main theme of existentialism?
    A.   Philosophy must focus on the individual in his or her confrontation with the world
    B.* Traditional and academic philosophy must be pressed into the service of real life
    C.   The world as found is irrational
    D.   The individual confronts the necessity to choose how he or she is to live

28. Which is *not* a theme of Albert Camus?
    A.   Each individual must spend life fighting the "plague"
    B.   A fundamental human need is clarity or understanding
    C.   Human beings are condemned to lives of futile labor
    D.* There is no God

29. Which is *not* a theme of Jean-Paul Sartre?
    A.   There is no objective standard of values
    B.   The individual is thrown into existence without any real reason for being
    C.   A human being has "being-for-itself"
    D.* There is no free will

30. For Sartre, the world lacks an ultimate rhyme or reason because
    A.   Human beings no longer perceive Being
    B.   Human beings are the product of evolution
    C.   Anguish clouds human understanding
    D.* God does not exist

31. Politically, Sartre considered himself a
    A.   Libertarian
    B.* Marxist
    C.   Neoconservative
    D.   "Know Nothing"

32. According to Jean-Paul Sartre, because there is no God
    A.* There is no objective good or evil
    B.   One no longer has any responsibility for making moral choices
    C.   Human beings are in fact slaves to random chance
    D.   Everything is truly permissible

33. Which is *not* a tenet of Husserl's investigation of phenomena?
    A.   One must "bracket" presuppositions
    B.   One must "exclude" one's presuppositions
    C.   One must perform the phenomenological reduction
    D.* One must consider what phenomena "represent" in the external world

34. Which is *not* a theme of Heidegger's *Being and Time*?
    A.   The absence of sense or meaning in life is the problem of human existence
    B.   A human being is "thrown into the world"
    C.   Humans are essentially temporal beings
    D.* We must think in a quiet, nonimpositional way to catch a glimpse of Being
         itself

35. Which is true of Heidegger?
    A.   He was uninterested in Eastern philosophy, especially in his later life
    B.* He was a Nazi
    C.   He used the term "bad faith" as part of his philosophical system
    D.   He wrote an early ad campaign for Cheerios

CHAPTER 8

The Pragmatic and Analytic Traditions

True/False

1. The philosophy of John Dewey is known as instrumentalism.
   T

2. Dewey equated the object with the thought about it, as had the German idealists.
   F

3. Dewey rejected the philosophy of "realism."
   T

4. Analytic philosophy developed primarily from the work of British philosophers.
   T

5. The purpose of analytic philosophy is to formulate answers to the "big" questions, such as whether God exists and what can be known for certain.
   F

6. The thesis that the concepts of mathematics can be defined in terms of concepts of logic, and that all mathematical truths can be proved from principles of formal logic, is known as logical positivism.
   F

7. Russell—at least for the major part of his life—said the world ultimately consists simply of things.
   F

8. Russell believed that complex propositions about the world must in principle be resolvable into simpler propositions.
T

9. Russell said that atomic facts are true or false depending on how people think about them.
F

10. For Russell, even our own sense-data cannot be truly known.
F

11. Phenomenalism maintained that you cannot possibly be mistaken about your sense-data.
T

12. Logical positivism concentrated on finding atomic propositions that would justify one's belief in God or in Reason as the fundamental cause of the universe.
F

13. The logical positivists said that because the tenets of metaphysics and theology cannot be empirically verified, they are meaningless.
T

14. Ludwig Wittgenstein studied under Bertrand Russell.
T

15. The Vienna Circle was formed in the 1920s so its members could pass around and eat small sausages.
F

16. The logical positivists of the Vienna Circle concentrated on analyzing the connection between language and the world.
F

17. Ludwig Wittgenstein, in his later philosophy, argued that we all speak private languages.
F

18. You really have to hand it to G. E. Moore for providing one of the shortest "refutations" of skepticism.
T

19. The foundationalist holds that a belief qualifies as knowledge only if it logically follows from incorrigible propositions.
T

20. Philosophers of mind generally begin with everyday psychological vocabulary and ask how it is to be analyzed or what it means.
T

21. The dualist says every existing thing, including abstract entities such as numbers and brotherhood, must be either physical or nonphysical.
F

22. The dualist must maintain that a person's physical and nonphysical components interact in some way.
F

23. Luisa Maria Oliva Sabuco de Nantes Barerra, as an interactionist dualist, reasoned that the connection between body and soul (mind) occurs throughout the brain.
T

24. The term "sense-data" as used by Bertrand Russell simply denotes the contents of what we see, hear, feel, taste, and so on, independent of any interpretation.
T

25. Philosophical behaviorist Gilbert Ryle maintained there was no such thing as a nonphysical mind.
T

26. Behaviorism, as Ryle expressed it, must set for itself the practical task of analyzing simple mental-state expressions into definite and finite sets of behaviors and behavioral propensities.
F

27. The identity theorist says only that thinking is *correlated with* or *involves* a neural process of the brain.
F

28. The behaviorist and identity theorist both accept the premise that a human being is an entirely physical organism.
T

29. The identity theory is a nondualistic theory.
T

30. The functionalist believes talk about beliefs and other mental phenomena must be reduced to statements about neurological processes.
F

31. If functionalism is correct, the possibility of a straightforward reductivist physicalism of "thoughts" expressed in the language of physics is most unlikely.
T

32. The problem of "intentionality" deals with such questions as who best knows the content of my own mental states—me, or an outside observer.
F

33. A problem for physicalist theories of mind is the question of how matter could be "conscious" of the world being "represented" to it.
T

34. Physicalist theories of the mind are said to be "complete" even though they cannot account convincingly for the irreducibly subjective nature of conscious states.
F

Multiple Choice

35. "Analyses are either incorrect or trivial." This is also referred to as
    A.   Logical positivism
    B.* The paradox of analysis
    C.   The "choice" theory of meaning
    D.   Language "taken on a holiday"

36. What was one attraction of the use of philosophical analysis?
    A.   It was able to verify certain elements in Hegel's theory of Absolute Idealism
    B.   It meant that all analysts would be working to analyze propositions about physical objects into propositions about sense-data
    C.* The method of analysis seemed to yield real progress in philosophy
    D.   The method was useful to the existentialist tradition

37. The "verifiability criterion of meaning" is associated most closely with
    A.   Ludwig Wittgenstein
    B.   Søren Kierkegaard
    C.* The Vienna Circle
    D.   Arthur Schopenhauer and Friedrich Nietzsche

38. The "picture theory of meaning" is associated with which of the following philosophers? (Hint: He rejected this theory in his later work.)
    A.   G. E. Moore
    B.   Bertrand Russell
    C.   W. V. O. Quine
    D.* Ludwig Wittgenstein

39. Which of the following is *not* true of John Dewey?
    A.   He was a champion of progressive education
    B.* He invented a classification system for libraries
    C.   He was one of the founders of the American Civil Liberties Union
    D.   He wrote a book entitled *The Quest for Certainty*

40. Which of the following would be rejected by logical positivists?
    A.   Metaphysical utterances are not meaningful empirical statements
    B.   Moral and value statements are empirically meaningless
    C.*   Absolute Idealism can be verified in principle
    D.   Apart from language, philosophy has no legitimate concern with the world

41. Which of the following did the later Wittgenstein *not* endorse?
    A.   The meanings of words do not lie inside the mind
    B.*   The meanings of words do lie inside the mind
    C.   The meanings of words are governed by their uses
    D.   The uses of words are governed by rules others can check

42. "It became generally accepted that there is no set of sense-data, the having of which logically entails that you are experiencing any given physical object." This quotation from the text helps explain the discrediting of
    A.   Wittgenstein's *Philosophical Investigations*
    B.   Nihilism
    C.*   Phenomenalism
    D.   Logical positivism

43. All of the following are analytic philosophers except
    A.   Russell
    B.   G. E. Moore
    C.*   Kierkegaard
    D.   Schlick

44. Resolving complex propositions into simpler ones is known as
    A.   Foundationalism
    B.*   Analysis
    C.   Synthesis
    D.   Positivism

45. Today, analytic philosophers
    A.   Agree that unverifiable propositions are meaningless
    B.   Agree that analysis is the (only) proper method of philosophy
    C.   Agree that foundationalism has been proven
    D.*   None of the above

46. The author of *Tractatus Logico-Philosophicus* was
    A.*   Wittgenstein
    B.   Russell
    C.   Quine
    D.   Rorty

47. Which philosopher was especially concerned with "the paradox of analysis"?
    A.   Wittgenstein
    B.*   G. E. Moore
    C.   Russell
    D.   Kierkegaard

48. According to most dualists, which of the following is false?
    A.   Physical and nonphysical things can both have temporal properties
    B.*   Mind is subject to the same principles that govern physical things
    C.   A human being is both a physical body and a nonphysical mind
    D.   The mental and physical components of a human being interact in some way

49. Which of the following is *not* expressly a reason for doubting that the mind is nonphysical?
    A.   The characterization problem
    B.   The individuation problem
    C.*   The intentionality problem
    D.   The interaction problem

50. Which of the following is *not* a tenet of the behaviorism of Gilbert Ryle?
    A.   There is no "ghost" within the machine
    B.   A person is only a complicated physical organism
    C.*   Thoughts and ideas are nonmaterial things defined by our behavior
    D.   References to someone's knowledge must be analyzed in terms of how a person is apt to behave in certain circumstances

51. Which of the following is *not* a claim made by the identity theory?
    A.   It is a materialistic theory
    B.   Each distinct mental state equates with one and only one brain state
    C.*   Philosophical behaviorism and the identity theory are essentially the same theories
    D.   A human being is an entirely physical organism

52. Which of the following correctly pairs a theory with an appropriate difficulty of that theory?
    A.*   Dualism and interactionism
    B.   Dualism and the final authority problem
    C.   The identity theory and interactionism
    D.   Behaviorism and the individuation problem

53. Which theory of mind would most likely subscribe to the following statement? "Though it is true that nothing nonphysical happens to you when you have a belief, that doesn't mean that we could somehow 'translate' statements about your beliefs into statements about neurological processes."
    A.   Idealism
    B.   Theoretical positivism
    C.   Dualism
    D.*   Functionalism

54. "How is it, then, that a purely physical system can have states that are propositional—that is, true or false?" Such a question deals with
    A.   The final authority problem
    B.   The problem of interactionism
    C.   The characterization problem
    D.* None of the above

55. According to the philosophical behaviorist, beliefs are
    A.   Physical things
    B.   Nonphysical things
    C.* Not things at all
    D.   None of the above

56. Philosophical behaviorists believe all of the following except
    A.   There are no nonphysical minds
    B.   Mental-state thing-words denote behavioral propensities and dispositions
    C.* Statements about a person's mental states can be translated into statements about a person's behaviors
    D.   A person's mental states are not the causes of his or her behavior

57. That mind-states are brain-states is the main thesis of
    A.   Behaviorism
    B.   Functionalism
    C.   Dualism
    D.* Identity theory

58. "Why can't two people share a single mind?" This question relates to the
    A.   Characterization problem
    B.* Individuation problem
    C.   Emergence problem
    D.   Dependency problem

CHAPTER 9

Moral Philosophy

True/False

1. Ethics is the psychological study of moral judgments.
   F

2. Ethical skepticism is the doctrine that moral knowledge is not possible.
   T

3. Subjectivism and ethical skepticism are in reality the same thing.
   F

4. Socrates believed that any sane person who possesses knowledge of the essence of virtue cannot fail to act virtuously.
   T

5. Plato taught that the Forms are perceptible to the senses of the virtuous person.
   F

6. According to Plato, the Form of the Good has objective reality.
   T

7. According to Plato, evil is unreal.
   T

8. Plato's moral philosophy, when compared with modern theories, is often said to be incomplete.
   F

9. Plato's moral philosophy is a version of ethical naturalism.
   F

10. Aesara, the Lucanian, claimed that the human soul had three parts: the mind, spiritedness, and desire.
   T

11. Aesara believed that the structure of the human soul provided insight into how society ought to be structured.
   T

12. Aristotle was the author of *The Nicomachean Ethics*.
   T

13. Our highest objective, according to Aristotle, is the attainment of pleasure.
   F

14. Aristotle said virtue is in large measure a matter of habit.
   T

15. Both Plato and Aristotle agreed on what the "four cardinal moral virtues" were.
   T

16. Aristotle's ethics were basically naturalistic.
   T

17. Epicureanism and Stoicism are both nonnaturalistic ethical philosophies.
   F

18. Diogenes was a Cynic.
   T

19. Epicurus believed the pleasant life comes only when all of your desires are satisfied.
   F

20. Aristippus espoused a hedonistic philosophy called Cyrenaicism, which said our lives should be dedicated to acquiring as many pleasures as possible.
   T

21. The Cynics were the historical precursors of the Stoics.
   T

22. The Stoics believed that everything that happened was in accord with what they called natural law.
   T

23. The essence of Stoic philosophy was something like, "control your attitude and you can control the world."
   F

24. Stoics had a duty to serve others.
    T

25. St. Augustine and Plato agreed with each other on the metaphysical status of evil.
    T

26. St. Augustine and the Stoics agreed with each other that the natural law is an impersonal rational principle that shapes the destiny of the cosmos.
    F

27. It followed for St. Augustine that since people, not God, create evil through their own free choice, then people can also directly create good.
    F

28. St. Hildegard of Bingen is described in the text as a "religious mystical philosopher."
    T

29. Hildegard said the vice of "immoderation" was like the wolf.
    T

30. During her lifetime, Hildegard's work was unknown to Catholic church officials.
    F

31. One of the components of Heloise's ethics was *disinterested love.*
    T

32. According to Heloise, the morality of an action is unconnected with the intention of the person who committed the act.
    F

33. For St. Thomas Aquinas, the natural law is the law of reason.
    T

34. Aquinas said there were two levels of virtues.
    T

35. The great theological achievement of St. Thomas Aquinas came in his attempted reconciliation of Platonism with Christianity.
    F

36. Epicurean ethical philosophy is a version of prescriptive egoism.
    T

37. Thomas Hobbes maintained that human beings, above all else, seek personal survival.
    T

38. Hobbes defined peace as a condition in which people *do not* harm each other.
F

39. For Hobbes, as well as for the Stoics, the natural law is a moral law.
F

40. In ethics, Hobbes is a descriptivist.
T

41. For David Hume, moral judgments are based on the principle of reason.
F

42. Hobbes and Hume agreed that the normal human being is a sympathetic creature.
F

43. Immanuel Kant held that moral principles can be revealed by scientific investigation.
F

44. For Kant, the supreme prescription of morality is to act always in such a way that you could, rationally, will the principle on which you act to be a universal law.
T

45. "If you want to be healthy, then live moderately!" is an example of a Kantian moral imperative.
F

46. Kant said what I should do I should do just because it is right.
T

47. For Kant, an act is morally good or not depending on the consequences of the act.
F

48. If we help someone because we are sympathetic to their plight, or are simply inclined to help them, such action, according to Kant, is of great moral worth.
F

49. Jeremy Bentham believed that the rightness of an action is identical with the happiness it produces as its consequence (with everyone considered).
T

50. Bentham said the pain and pleasure an act produces can be evaluated solely with reference to quantitative criteria.
T

51. Another name for utilitarianism is "universalistic ethical hedonism."
T

52. The "calculus of pleasure" is associated with the utilitarian John Stuart Mill.
F

53. Both Bentham and Mill believed that some pleasures are inherently better than others.
F

54. Mill said the most desirable of two pleasures (the one of higher quality) is the one to which most who have experienced both give a decided preference.
T

55. Moral judgments, for utilitarians, are in effect types of factual judgments about how much happiness certain actions produce.
T

56. The "paradox of hedonism" is that pursuit of higher-quality pleasures produces a craving for lower-quality pleasures.
F

57. For Friedrich Nietzsche, Christian ethics was "slave morality."
T

Multiple Choice

58. Who is most likely to have written this? "Take any action allowed to be vicious. . . . The vice entirely escapes you, as long as you consider the object. You never can find it, till you turn your reflexion into your own breast, and find a sentiment of disapprobation. . . ."
    A.   Thomas Hobbes
    B.*   David Hume
    C.   St. Thomas Aquinas
    D.   Hildegard of Bingen

59. Who is most likely to have written this? ". . . for we always choose [happiness] for itself, and never for the sake of something else. . . . But there must also be a full term of years for this exercise [in developing virtue]; for one swallow or one fine day does not make a spring. . . ."
    A.   Thomas Hobbes
    B.   Epictetus
    C.*   Aristotle
    D.   David Hume

60. Who is most likely to have written this? "Do not seek to have everything that happens happen as you wish, but wish for everything to happen as it actually does happen, and your life will be serene. . . ."
    A.   Thomas Hobbes
    B.* Epictetus
    C.   Aristotle
    D.   St. Augustine

61. Who is most likely to have written this? ". . . man's ultimate happiness consists in wisdom, based on the consideration of divine things. It is therefore evident by way of induction that man's ultimate happiness consists solely in the contemplation of God. . . ."
    A.   Thomas Hobbes
    B.* St. Thomas Aquinas
    C.   David Hume
    D.   Aristotle

62. Who is most likely to have written this? "So that in the nature of man, we find three principal causes of quarrel. First, competition; secondly, diffidence; thirdly, glory. . . . [T]he life of man [is] solitary, poor, nasty, brutish, and short."
    A.* Thomas Hobbes
    B.   St. Thomas Aquinas
    C.   David Hume
    D.   Aesara the Lucanian

63. Who is most likely to have written this? "When, therefore, we maintain that pleasure is the end, we do not mean the pleasures of profligates and those that consist in sensuality. . . . Of all this the beginning and the greatest good is prudence."
    A.   St. Hildegard of Bingen
    B.* Epicurus
    C.   Aristotle
    D.   Heloise

64. "The moral standards people subscribe to differ from culture to culture." This is called
    A.   Subjectivism
    B.* Cultural relativism
    C.   Ethical relativism
    D.   Ethical egoism

65. According to Plato, when our appetites are ruled by reason, we exhibit the virtue of
    A.   Tolerance
    B.   Courage
    C.* Temperance
    D.   Wisdom

66. Which is *not* a doctrine of Aristotle?
    A.   Human good is defined by human nature
    B.   There are two different kinds of virtues
    C.   Specific moral virtues are the means between extremes
    D.*   The right kind of pleasure constitutes happiness

67. According to Epicurus, which desire is never prudent to satisfy?
    A.*   The desire for fame
    B.   The desire for shelter
    C.   The desire for sexual gratification
    D.   The desire for food

68. Which of the following is *not* considered a Stoic?
    A.   Zeno of Citium
    B.   Cicero
    C.*   Epicurus
    D.   Marcus Aurelius

69. Which of the following is *not* true of St. Augustine?
    A.   He drew on the Neoplatonic philosophy of Plotinus
    B.*   He said the eternal law is written in the heart of men, but not women
    C.   He said moral evil is a case of misdirected love
    D.   He drew on the philosophy of Plato

70. Which group is in the correct historical order?
    A.*   St. Augustine, St. Hildegard of Bingen, St. Thomas Aquinas
    B.   Plato, St. Thomas Aquinas, Marcus Aurelius
    C.   Cicero, Aristotle, St. Thomas Aquinas
    D.   Thomas Hobbes, St. Thomas Aquinas, David Hume

71. Which of the following is *not* true of Heloise?
    A.   She was a French philosopher and poet
    B.   Pierre Abelard was her philosophy teacher
    C.*   Heloise became pregnant by Abelard and named the child Sextant
    D.   Her uncle had Abelard castrated

72. According to Aquinas, which of the following is out of place in the group?
    A.   Courage
    B.   Temperance
    C.*   Hope
    D.   Justice

73. According to Hobbes, justice and morality begin and end with
    A.   The individual
    B.   The church
    C.*   The sovereign state
    D.   Justice and morality do not truly exist

74. Which of the following is *not* a tenet held by Hobbes?
    A.*   Natural laws are moral prescriptions
    B.   Good and evil are defined subjectively
    C.   Justice and injustice have to do with breaking agreements
    D.   Natural rights do not morally prohibit any activity

75. Which claim would David Hume have agreed with?
    A.   Moral principles are divine edicts
    B.   Moral principles are the "offspring of reason"
    C.   Moral principles do not exist
    D.*   Moral principles are expressions of a particular kind of pleasure

76. Which of the following tenets would *not* be held by Immanuel Kant?
    A.   Reason alone can determine whether or not an act is morally right
    B.   One must treat rational beings in every instance as ends and never just as means
    C.*   There are no exceptionless moral principles
    D.   What is within your control is the intent with which you act, not the consequences of the act

77. Consider the following: "The morally best act is the one that produces, compared with all possible alternative acts, the greatest amount of happiness with everyone considered." Who would subscribe to this assertion?
    A.   Aristotle
    B.   Friedrich Nietzsche
    C.*   Jeremy Bentham
    D.   Immanuel Kant

78. Which of the following offered a defense of the utilitarian notion that it is the general happiness one should aim to promote by observing that moral principles are impartial in singling out no one (not even myself) for preferential treatment?
    A.   Jeremy Bentham
    B.*   John Stuart Mill
    C.   Henry Sidgwick
    D.   David Hume

79. "A value-neutral investigation into the logical relationships of moral value judgments" is called
    A.   The categorical imperative
    B.   Relativism
    C.*   Metaethics
    D.   Applied ethics

80. Who is most likely to have written the following? "Act as though the maxim of your action were by your will to become a universal law of nature."
    A. John Stuart Mill
    B. Jeremy Bentham
    C.* Immanuel Kant
    D. Jean-Paul Sartre

81. Who is most likely to have written the following? "An action then may be said to be conformable . . . to utility . . . when the tendency it has to augment the happiness of the community is greater than any it has to diminish it."
    A. Friedrich Nietzsche
    B.* Jeremy Bentham
    C. Immanuel Kant
    D. St. Thomas Aquinas

82. Who is most likely to have written the following? "A morality of the ruling group, however, is most alien and embarrassing to the present taste in the severity of its principle that one has duties only to one's peers; that against beings of a lower rank, against everything alien, one may behave as one pleases or 'as the heart desires,' and in any case 'beyond good and evil.'"
    A.* Friedrich Nietzsche
    B. Jeremy Bentham
    C. Immanuel Kant
    D. Starbuck Coffee

CHAPTER 10

Political Philosophy

True/False

1. According to Plato, the lowest element in the soul corresponds in the well-ordered state to the class of police-soldiers.
   F

2. For Plato, the ideal state is governed by a ruling elite.
   T

3. Plato believed that the best form of government would eventually degenerate into a timocracy.
   T

4. For both Plato and Aristotle, the state is an organism, a living being.
   T

5. For Aristotle, a state is good to the extent that it is well-ordered.
   F

6. Aristotle thought that states may be good or bad irrespective of the form of government.
   T

7. Aristotle, unlike Plato, was an egalitarian.
   F

8. In order to determine what the purpose of the state ought to be, Aristotle considered what the purpose of existing states actually is.
   T

9. Cicero said the natural law of reason is eternal and universal.
   T

10. According to contemporary philosopher Michael Walzer, the use of military force by one state on another can be justified only as a response to aggression, and (except for a few unusual cases) not for any other end.
T

11. For Aquinas, the sole purpose of the state is to take "the power to do hurt" from those who are wicked.
F

12. Thomas Hobbes maintained that the natural law is the law of God.
F

13. Without the state, Hobbes said, people live in a tranquil "state of nature" that encourages laziness and lack of productivity.
F

14. Hobbes defined justice and injustice as the keeping and breaking of covenants.
T

15. According to Hobbes, the Leviathan is prone to act unjustly toward its subjects.
F

16. Hobbes said the only alternative to anarchy is dictatorship.
T

17. Hobbes, along with John Locke and Jean-Jacques Rousseau, can be described as a contractarian theorist.
T

18. Montesquieu said the judiciary should be a separate branch of government.
T

19. Locke agreed with Hobbes on the content of the natural law.
F

20. For both Hobbes and Locke, the subject gives up his rights to (that is, over to) the state in return for security.
F

21. Locke believed people have a natural right to property.
T

22. Niccolò Machiavelli wrote that Christianity had made men feeble and needy of the absolute rule of a prince.
T

23. In his advice to the prince, Machiavelli said that princes who wish to survive had to learn how to be loved but not feared.
F

24. Locke, unlike Hobbes, called for a division of governmental authority.
T

25. Catharine Trotter Cockburn published a number of philosophical pamphlets defending the philosophy of Thomas Hobbes.
F

26. For Jean-Jacques Rousseau, the "state of nature" was a time of innocence, goodness, and happiness.
T

27. According to Rousseau, the "general will" is always the will of the majority.
F

28. Rousseau maintained that the citizens of the state have the right to terminate the social contract at any time.
T

29. Mary Wollstonecraft was particularly pleased with Jean-Jacques Rousseau's view of women.
F

30. Wollstonecraft argued that women were as capable as men of attaining the virtues of wisdom and rationality if only society would allow those virtues to be cultivated.
T

31. The original U.S. Constitution was directed toward establishing law and order and not toward guaranteeing natural rights.
T

32. According to the text, the U.S. Supreme Court must determine what rights have been incorporated into the U.S. Constitution.
T

33. In *Roe v. Wade* , the U.S. Supreme Court upheld a woman's right to abortion as included within the right to privacy.
T

34. *Utopian* theories are theories about perfect societies.
T

35. Harriet Taylor was closely associated with Karl Marx on both a personal and professional capacity.
F

36. Taylor believed that all differences between men and women (except perhaps for some difference in physical strength) were socially created.
T

37. Taylor argued that women were not yet ready to be given the right to vote.
F

38. Adam Smith is famous for his "invisible hand" explanation.
T

39. Like Rousseau, John Stuart Mill viewed a state as an organic entity separate and distinct from the sum of the people in it.
F

40. Both Mill and Rousseau rejected Locke's theory that people have God-given natural rights.
T

41. Mill was an exponent both of utilitarianism and liberalism.
T

42. The French doctrine of *couverture* is the idea that women's interests are "covered" or taken care of by the men who by law are in charge of them.
T

43. Anna Wheeler was an Irish feminist.
T

44. Utopians considered themselves implementers of Bentham's utilitarian principle, the greatest happiness for the greatest number.
T

45. For utopians like Saint-Simone, one of government's responsibilities was to help individuals develop a benevolent attitude toward one another.
T

46. Prince Piotr Kropotkin was a Russian anarchist much influenced by Charles Darwin.
T

47. For Karl Marx, human history consisted of successive stages of development of various means of production.
T

48. According to Marx, the dialectic process of class struggle is both inevitable and eternal.
   F

49. Mikhail Bakunin advocated the violent overthrow of all government.
   T

50. According to Marx, capitalism inevitably sows the seeds of its own destruction.
   T

51. Marx could be described as a revisionist or evolutionary socialist.
   F

Multiple Choice

52. Which of the following is *not* one of the classes of Plato's ideal state?
   A.   Craftspersons
   B.*   Judges
   C.   Police-soldiers
   D.   Governing class

53. According to Plato, a society that cannot hold wealth in honor and at the same time establish self-control in its citizens degenerates into a
   A.*   Democracy
   B.   Plutocracy
   C.   Aristocracy
   D.   Tyranny

54. According to Plato, which of the following is *not* a characteristic of the ruling class?
   A.   Members do not have private property
   B.   Reproduction among its members is arranged
   C.*   Care of each guardian's children is the responsibility of that guardian
   D.   The guardians are trained for soldiering

55. According to Aristotle, proper rule by the many is called a polity; improper rule by the many is called a (an)
   A.   Tyranny
   B.   Oligarchy
   C.*   Democracy
   D.   Republic

56. Aquinas said the fundamental principles of morality, as apprehended by us in our conscience and practical reasoning, is called
   A.   The eternal law
   B.   The divine law
   C.*   The natural law
   D.   Human law

57. According to Aquinas, which of the following is *not* one of the conditions of a just war?
   A.   The ruler under whom the war is to be fought must have authority to do so
   B.   The cause must be just
   C.   Those making war must intend to achieve some good or avoid some evil
   D.* The war must be supported by 66 2/3% of the people

58. Which of the following is *not* one of Hobbes's natural "laws"?
   A.* Men have a right to break the covenants they make
   B.   We should be content to have only so much liberty as we are prepared to grant others
   C.   Seek peace as best you can
   D.   If you can't find peace, defend yourself

59. Which of the following is *not* true of Hobbes's Leviathan?
   A.   It is the central sovereign power
   B.* It can rightfully compel a subject to take his or her life
   C.   It has no legal or moral obligation to its subjects
   D.   There can be no contract or covenant between the Leviathan and its subjects

60. Which of the following is *not* true of John Locke and his political beliefs?
   A.   His political ideas have become part of American popular political thought
   B.   We are all made by God and are his "property"
   C.* A state is legitimate only if all its subjects give explicit consent to its formation
   D.   People have a right to whatever things they "mix their labor with"

61. Who is most likely to have written this? "Each of us places in common his person and all his power under the supreme direction of the general will. . . . this act of association produces a . . . public person. . . ."
   A.   Plato
   B.* Jean-Jacques Rousseau
   C.   Thomas Aquinas
   D.   Mary Wollstonecraft

62. Who is most likely to have written this? "The great and chief end, therefore, of men uniting into commonwealths, and putting themselves under government, is the preservation of their property."
   A.   Plato
   B.   Jean-Jacques Rousseau
   C.   Mary Wollstonecraft
   D.* John Locke

63. Who is most likely to have written this? "A LAW OF NATURE . . . is a precept or general rule, found out by reason, by which a man is forbidden to do that which is destructive of his life or takes away the means of preserving the same. . . ."
    A.   Aristotle
    B.   Plato
    C.*   Thomas Hobbes
    D.   Niccolò Machiavelli

64. Who is most likely to have written this? ". . . the best men must cohabit with the best women in as many cases as possible and the worst with the worst in the fewest, and . . . the offspring of the one must be reared and that of the other not. . . ."
    A.   Aristotle
    B.*   Plato
    C.   Mary Wollstonecraft
    D.   John Locke

65. Who is most likely to have written this? "But should it be proved that woman is naturally weaker than man, whence does it follow that it is natural for her to labour to become still weaker than nature intended her to be?"
    A.   Aristotle
    B.*   Mary Wollstonecraft
    C.   Thomas Hobbes
    D.   John Locke

66. Who is most likely to have written this? "Society as a whole is splitting up more and more into two great hostile camps, into two great classes directly facing each other: Bourgeoisie and Proletariat."
    A.*   Karl Marx
    B.   Adam Smith
    C.   John Stuart Mill
    D.   Mary Wollstonecraft

67. Who is most likely to have written this? "That principle is, that the sole end for which mankind are warranted, individually or collectively, in interfering with the liberty of action of any of their number, is self-protection."
    A.   Karl Marx
    B.   Plato
    C.   Aristotle
    D.*   John Stuart Mill

68. Anna Wheeler and William Thompson wrote a response to James Mill, the father of John Stuart Mill, in which they argued that
    A.   The French doctrine of *couverture* ought to be instituted in the United States
    B.   Children under 15 ought to have the right to vote
    C.*   Denying rights to women was inconsistent with the philosophy of utilitarianism
    D.   Slavery was morally justified under certain circumstances

69. Which of the following is *not* considered a utopian?
    A.   Claude Saint-Simone
    B.* Harriet Taylor
    C.   Robert Owen
    D.   Charles Fourier

70. Who is called "the father of anarchism"?
    A.* Pierre Joseph Proudhon
    B.   Prince Piotr Kropotkin
    C.   Karl Marx
    D.   Adam Smith

CHAPTER 11

Recent Moral and Political Philosophy

True/False

1. G. E. Moore was an analytic philosopher.
   T

2. Moore held that "goodness" is a complex concept that can be broken down or "analyzed" into simpler constituents.
   F

3. Moore believed that good, or goodness, is a nonnatural property.
   T

4. "First-order thinking" is called metaethics.
   F

5. Moore said the good things we can really hope to obtain are personal affection and aesthetic enjoyments.
   T

6. In his analysis of ethical terms, W. D. Ross agreed with Kant that our *prima facie* duties are absolute duties.
   F

7. The importance of Moore and Ross to philosophy has been primarily in their metaethical theories.
   T

8. Both Ross and Kant accepted versions of deontological ethics.
   T

9. The emotivists said that moral judgments have no factual meaning whatsoever.
   T

10. According to the contemporary British linguistic philosopher R. M. Hare, the function of moral discourse is to express or influence attitudes (a view reminiscent of the emotivist position).
    F

11. David Hume maintained that one cannot deduce an "ought" from an "is."
    T

12. Both Phillipa Foot and John Searle accept the idea that moral evaluations are logically independent of the descriptive premises on which (in everyday conversation) they are based.
    F

13. Both John Rawls and Thomas Hobbes proposed a contractarian theory of justice.
    T

14. According to John Rawls, if a society's principles of justice are to be reasonable and justifiable, they must be selected through a procedure that is fair.
    T

15. The "veil of ignorance" and "original position" are hypothetical states or conditions.
    T

16. Rawls's two principles of justice are hierarchical (that is, one takes precedence over the other).
    T

17. For Rawls, an unequal distribution of the various assets of society can never be truly just.
    F

18. According to Rawls, the most important good is self-respect.
    T

19. Rawls draws his social ethics from a concept of natural law.
    F

20. In his recent work, Rawls characterizes justice as a freestanding *political conception* rather than as a *comprehensive value system*.
    T

21. Robert Nozick uses an "invisible hand explanation" in trying to show how a minimal state can arise without violating people's rights.
T

22. According to Nozick, justice sometimes requires the redistribution of the goods of society.
F

23. For Nozick, utilitarianism provides an adequate basis for the concept of animal rights.
F

24. John Locke would agree with Nozick that taking from the rich without compensation and giving to the poor is never just.
T

25. According to Rawls's theory of justice, taking from the rich and giving to the poor is just if it is to the greater good of the aggregate, even if it compromises someone's liberty.
F

26. Communitarians believe that the common good is defined by one's society or "community" and that the attainment of this common good arguably has priority over individual liberty.
T

27. Contemporary proponents of virtue ethics include Alasdair MacIntyre and Philippa Foot.
T

28. For Michael Sandel, John Rawls's principle of equal liberty is subordinate to the good of one's community, described by Sandel as an intersubjective or collective self.
T

29. Alasdair MacIntyre disagreed with Aristotle, who said that human nature must be conceived in terms of its potentialities.
F

30. MacIntyre distinguishes between the excellences or goods that are internal to a practice and those that are external to it.
T

31. According to Herbert Marcuse, the working class in advanced capitalist societies is no longer a force for radical social change.
T

32. Marcuse, though a Marxist philosopher, denied that a society without war, exploitation, repression, and poverty was possible.
F

33. Fascism is a kind of totalitarianism.
T

34. According to the text, the *equivalence thesis* has to do with whether it is really true that letting people die of starvation is as bad as killing them.
T

35. Feminist thought is often divided into two "waves," the first wave ending in 1922 with the vote for women in the United States.
T

36. Mary Wollstonecraft argued that a woman's central ambition ought to be to learn how to "inflame the passions" of men.
F

37. The utilitarian philosopher Harriet Taylor was a proponent of women's suffrage.
T

38. Simone de Beauvoir argued that women's status as Other was unique to women.
F

39. Simone de Beauvoir thought it was important to preserve the myth of women's "mystery."
F

40. Kate Millett believed that our society is a patriarchy.
T

41. If you endorse *androgyny*, you believe that male and female characteristics should be combined.
T

42. Ann Ferguson held that individuals should be androgynous.
T

43. Joyce Trebilcot argued that individuals should be able to choose to be masculine, feminine, or androgynous.
T

44. Marilyn Frye argues that the whole system of gender is really one of power.
T

45. Sara Ruddick argues that motherhood is a bad idea.
    F

46. Gloria Steinem was the founder of *Ms.* magazine.
    T

47. Shulamith Firestone could be seen as a kind of biological determinist.
    T

48. Carol Gilligan argued that women develop differently from men and that their moral intuitions and perspectives are different as well.
    T

49. Gilligan maintained that issues of abstract justice and rights are primary considerations in the way women reason morally.
    F

50. Nel Noddings is a proponent of what she calls "the ethics of caring."
    T

51. All feminist ethicists are alike in making concerns for rights and justice merely secondary.
    F

52. Susan Moller Okin argued that the theories of Rawls, Nozick, MacIntyre, Walzer, and Sandel have all been sensitive to the place of gender in moral and political philosophy.
    F

53. Okin's analysis of the family found it was, by and large, an unjust institution.
    T

54. Deontological ethics really means the same thing as consequentialist ethics.
    F

Multiple Choice

55. Which of the following is an emotivist?
    A.* C. L. Stevenson
    B. G. E. Moore
    C. W. D. Ross
    D. Susan Moller Okin

56. Who is most likely to have written the following? "... 'good' has no definition because it is simple and has no parts."
    A.   Sara Ruddick
    B.   John Stuart Mill
    C.   W. D. Ross
    D.* G. E. Moore

57. What is the so-called "naturalist fallacy"?
    A.   Defining the word "good"
    B.   The basis of contractarian theory
    C.* Deducing an "ought" from an "is"
    D.   None of the above

58. Who is most likely to have written this? "And yet this society is irrational as a whole. Its productivity is destructive of the free development of human needs and faculties, its peace manifested by the constant threat of war.... Men must come to see it and to find their way from false to true consciousness."
    A.* Herbert Marcuse
    B.   Robert Nozick
    C.   John Rawls
    D.   Harriet Taylor

59. Who is most likely to have written this? "The principle of fairness ... is objectionable and unacceptable. ... One cannot, whatever one's purposes, just act so as to give people benefits and then demand (or seize) payment."
    A.   Herbert Marcuse
    B.   Benito Mussolini
    C.   John Rawls
    D.* Robert Nozick

60. Who is most likely to have written this? "... the principles of justice are the result of a fair agreement or bargain."
    A.   Herbert Marcuse
    B.   Marilyn Frye
    C.* John Rawls
    D.   Robert Nozick

61. Which of the following is a tenet *not* held by Nozick?
    A.   His is an entitlement concept of social justice
    B.   The state is seen as a night watchman
    C.* Someone else's not providing you with the things you greatly need violates your rights
    D.   Individuals have rights

62. Which of the following would agree that "all social goods are to be distributed equally unless an unequal distribution is to everyone's advantage"?
    A.   Robert Nozick
    B.*   John Rawls
    C.   Alasdair MacIntyre
    D.   Adam Smith

63. According to Rawls, a well-ordered state must meet each of these conditions except
    A.   Its members must know and accept the same principles of social justice
    B.   The basic social institutions generally must satisfy the principles of social justice
    C.   The basic social institutions generally must be known to satisfy the principles of social justice
    D.*   The basic principles of social justice must be enforced by Constitutional provision

64. Rawls's "original position" is roughly equivalent to all of the following except
    A.   The initial situation
    B.*   A night-watchman state
    C.   The state of nature
    D.   Operating behind a veil of ignorance

65. Which of the following is a view of Rawls?
    A.   Social goods should always be distributed equally
    B.*   A person's liberty cannot be sacrificed for the common good
    C.   Unequal distribution of wealth can never be to everyone's benefit
    D.   The principles of social justice must, in the end, be determined by utilitarian considerations

66. Which of the following is *not* a view of Nozick?
    A.   The just state protects rights
    B.   Any state that does more than the minimal state violates rights
    C.   The minimal state is inspiring
    D.*   The just state ensures the equal distribution of goods

67. Contemporary philosopher Michael Walzer argues that any full account of how social goods ought to be distributed will be "thick." What is "thick"?
    A.   An abstract and universal point of view
    B.*   A view framed within a specific culture
    C.   A necessarily very complicated political view
    D.   Having some disease

68. For Alasdair MacIntyre, the ultimate alternative to Aristotle was
    A.   John Stuart Mill
    B.   John Rawls
    C.*   Friedrich Nietzsche
    D.   Karl Marx

69. Harriet Taylor grounded her ideas in
    A.   Kantian theory
    B.   Virtue theory
    C.* Utilitarian theory
    D.   None of the above

70. Polyandrogyny is a system in which
    A.   Everyone has both male and female characteristics
    B.* People choose which characteristics to have
    C.   Male and female characteristics have been eliminated
    D.   None of the above

71. Kate Millett thought that
    A.* Every avenue of power in the society is within male hands
    B.   Motherhood could be the means of transforming society
    C.   Pornography is the most important issue women face
    D.   Only A and C above

72. Marilyn Frye suggested that
    A.   Clothes do not make the man
    B.* Clothing is one way we mark and announce our status in society
    C.   Appearance is less important than what is inside the individual
    D.   None of the above

73. Nancy Chodorow thought that our child-rearing practices lead to
    A.* Little boys emphasizing autonomy and distance
    B.   Little girls emphasizing autonomy and distance
    C.   An androgynous culture
    D.   None of the above

74. "Maternal thinking" is something that
    A.   Only women can achieve
    B.* Anyone who acts as a mother can achieve
    C.   Is an unreachable ideal
    D.   None of the above

75. Susan Moller Okin argued against the idea that people own what they produce, and
    that such a right takes precedence over other rights. That is reduced to nonsense ,
    she said, when it is observed that under that principle women "own" everyone they
    give birth to. Okin was arguing against the views of which philosopher?
    A.   John Rawls
    B.* Robert Nozick
    C.   Alasdair MacIntyre
    D.   Michael Sandel

CHAPTER 12

Philosophy and Belief in God

True/False

1. If you believe you should love your neighbor because God said you should, you have committed yourself to a stand against ethical naturalism.
   T

2. The philosopher of religion makes religious assumptions in order to better understand and evaluate religious beliefs.
   F

3. St. Anselm's consideration of the question of God's existence began with the premise that by "God" is meant "the greatest being conceivable."
   T

4. St. Anselm tried to demonstrate that it is self-contradictory to deny that God exists.
   T

5. St. Anselm is the father of the "teleological argument" for God's existence.
   F

6. St. Anselm's argument for God's existence is a reductio proof.
   T

7. Gaunilo's "perfect island" argument was designed to support the ontological argument.
   F

8. St. Thomas Aquinas regarded the ontological argument as valid.
   F

9. Aquinas's first three proofs of God's existence are versions of the cosmological argument.
    T

10. Aquinas rejected the so-called "moral argument" as being unable to prove God's existence.
    F

11. The ontological argument for God's existence is predicated on the observation that natural things have a plan or design.
    F

12. According to Aquinas, philosophy cannot prove anything known by faith.
    F

13. According to Aquinas, it is philosophically untenable that a chain of causes could go back infinitely.
    F

14. Julian of Norwich was one of the greatest mystics of all time.
    T

15. Julian denied that there is any meaningful distinction between the validity of knowledge derived through rationalistic philosophy and the validity of that derived through mystical revelations made directly to our soul.
    T

16. In his first proof of God's existence, René Descartes argues that God is the cause of Descartes's idea of God.
    T

17. In his second proof of God's existence, Descartes argues that the only thing adequate to sustain his own existence is God.
    T

18. Descartes's third proof is a version of the cosmological argument.
    F

19. Descartes believed that existence is a perfection.
    T

20. For Gottfried Wilhelm, Baron von Leibniz, the basic constituent of reality was an indivisible *physical* particle called a monad.
    F

21. Leibniz appealed to the principle of sufficient reason for his proof of God's existence.
    T

22. Leibniz argued that God was a necessary being.
    T

23. Leibniz rejected theodicies as man's meddling in divine affairs.
    F

24. David Hume's empiricist epistemological principles (if valid) rule out the possibility of any meaningful ontological argument.
    T

25. Hume criticized the teleological argument in part as setting up a false analogy that likened the universe to a human contrivance.
    T

26. Despite his critique of traditional proofs for God's existence, Hume was a staunch believer in divine action (miracles).
    F

27. Immanuel Kant doubted God's existence.
    F

28. Kant maintained that existence is not a perfection or any other kind of characteristic.
    T

29. Kant thought belief in God's existence was rationally justified for any moral agent.
    T

30. Kant in essence rejected the cosmological, teleological, and ontological arguments for God's existence, but affirmed the moral argument for God's existence.
    T

31. According to John Henry Newman, we are simply unable to doubt God's existence given the experience of conscience.
    T

32. For Søren Kierkegaard, salvation is possible only through a leap of faith—a nonintellectual commitment to God.
    T

33. The Scopes "monkey trial" took place in the 1920s.
    T

34. The Institute for Creation Research, located in California, subscribes to a "theistic evolutionary" viewpoint.
F

35. Friedrich Nietzsche said "God is dead" because he believed that God had once existed but now no longer existed.
F

36. According to William James, our convictions are determined not by pure reason but by our "passional nature."
T

37. James's philosophy was a type of pragmatism.
T

38. When it came to matters as important as whether God existed, James insisted that we avoid error at all cost.
F

39. James's argument for belief in God seemed to some believers as nothing more than a gamble rather than a true acceptance of God.
T

40. Rudolph Carnap said he rejected all philosophical questions because they were not subject to the verifiability principle of logical positivism.
T

41. Alvin Plantinga argues that the theist may accept the belief in God as a "basic belief," a belief that is rational to hold without supporting evidence.
T

42. Mary Daly argued that the image of God as Father perpetuates the artificial polarization of human qualities into the traditional sexual stereotypes.
T

43. Daly maintained that God was not a noun, but an adjective.
F

Multiple Choice

44. Who is most likely to have written this? "The existence of God can be proved in five ways."
   A.   St. Anselm
   B.*   St. Thomas Aquinas
   C.   Immanuel Kant
   D.   Leibniz

45. Who is most likely to have written this? "But there must be a sufficient reason for contingent truths . . . and the sufficient or final reason must be outside of the sequence or series. . . . And thus it is that the final reason of things must be found in a necessary substance. . . ."
    A.   St. Anselm
    B.   St. Thomas Aquinas
    C.   Immanuel Kant
    D.* Leibniz

46. Who is most likely to have written this? "This was a rich, full, sweet vision: that God's throne is in our soul, because it is God's pleasure to reign in our understanding."
    A.   Immanuel Kant
    B.   Leibniz
    C.* Julian of Norwich
    D.   Descartes

47. Who is most likely to have written this? "But surely that than which a greater cannot be thought cannot exist merely in the mind. For if it exists merely in the mind, it can be thought to exist also in reality which is greater."
    A.* St. Anselm
    B.   Julian of Norwich
    C.   St. Thomas Aquinas
    D.   Leibniz

48. Who is most likely to have written this? "When, therefore, I think a being as the supreme reality, without any defect, the question still remains whether it exists or not."
    A.   St. Anselm
    B.   St. Thomas Aquinas
    C.* Immanuel Kant
    D.   Leibniz

49. Who is most likely to have written this? "For although the idea of substance is within me owing to the fact that I am substance, nevertheless I could not have the idea of an infinite substance—since I am finite—if it had not proceeded from some substance which was veritably infinite."
    A.   David Hume
    B.* René Descartes
    C.   Mary Daly
    D.   Immanuel Kant

50. Who is most likely to have written this? "Add to this that in tracing an eternal succession of objects it seems absurd to inquire for a general cause or first author. How can anything that exists from eternity have a cause, since that relation implies a priority in time and a beginning of existence?"
    A.* David Hume
    B.   René Descartes
    C.   Leibniz
    D.   Immanuel Kant

51. Who is most likely to have written this? "'God' can be used oppressively against women in a number of ways. . . . [I]t occurs in an overt manner when theologians proclaim women's subordination to be God's will."
    A.   St. Thomas Aquinas
    B.   Nietzsche
    C.   Immanuel Kant
    D.* Mary Daly

52. Who is most likely to have written this? "When anyone tells me, that he saw a dead man restored to life, I immediately consider with myself, whether it be more probable that this person should either deceive or be deceived, or that the fact which he relates should really have happened."
    A.   Descartes
    B.   Leibniz
    C.   Kant
    D.* Hume

53. That the denial of God's existence is a self-contradiction is a fundamental premise of the
    A.   Cosmological argument
    B.   Teleological argument
    C.* Ontological argument
    D.   Moral argument

54. Gaunilo was a contemporary of
    A.* Anselm
    B.   Aquinas
    C.   Descartes
    D.   Kant

55. The system of which philosopher was declared by Pope Leo XIII to be the official Catholic philosophy?
    A.   Anselm
    B.* Aquinas
    C.   Descartes
    D.   Albertus Magnus

56. The principle of sufficient reason was used by which philosopher in a proof that God exists?
    A.   Descartes
    B.* Leibniz
    C.   Gaunilo
    D.   Hume

57. Theodicy is
    A.   The study of different religious belief systems
    B.* The defense of God's goodness in view of apparent evil
    C.   The name given to the collected proofs of God's existence
    D.   Another name for philosophy of religion

58. That the dispute between theists and atheists is in certain respects merely a verbal dispute is an idea proposed by
    A.   Descartes
    B.* Hume
    C.   Kant
    D.   None of the above

59. According to the logical positivists, the utterance "God exists" is
    A.   Definitely false
    B.   Probably false
    C.* Meaningless
    D.   Probably true

60. Which philosopher proposed a famous wager about the stakes in believing in God?
    A.   John Henry Newman
    B.* Blaise Pascal
    C.   Nietzsche
    D.   Mary Daly

CHAPTER 13

An Era of Suspicion

True/False

1. Jürgen Habermas is a proponent of "critical theory."
    T

2. Habermas proposed a theory of communicative competence that involved what he called a universal phenomenology of consciousness.
    F

3. The Frankfurt School was a training center for Nazis during World War II.
    F

4. Michel Foucault in his later writing rejected the archaeological approach of his philosophy in favor of a genealogical approach.
    T

5. For Foucault, the genealogical approach committed the researcher to a universal theory of the human subject.
    F

6. Foucault died of AIDS.
    T

7. *Semiotics* may be defined as the "science of signs."
    T

8. Jacques Derrida is associated with the theory called deconstruction.
    T

9. In the view of American philosopher Richard Rorty, the philosophy of Heidegger has great public usefulness.
    F

10. Rorty would describe himself as a pragmatist.
    T

11. For Rorty, standards such as evidence, reasonableness, knowledge, and truth are "starting points" relative to a given culture.
    T

12. According to the text, feminism has been a largely white, middle-class phenomenon.
    T

13. Lorraine Code is a feminist epistemologist.
    T

14. Feminist epistemologists generally emphasize that ideal knowers are purely rational, fully informed, and completely objective.
    F

15. Ecofeminists see a connection between the domination of women and the domination of nature.
    T

16. Ecofeminist Val Plumwood would best be described as a "mind/body dualist."
    F

17. The problem with liberal individualism, according to Plumwood, is that it views nature as a resource.
    T

18. Plumwood argues that the central task of environmental ethics is to prove that animals and other nonhuman living things have rights.
    F

Multiple Choice

19. According to Habermas,
    A.   Modern technocratic society has developed ethics to a high degree
    B.   The so-called positivistic sciences have the only correct way of looking at the world
    C.* Positivistic sciences cannot provide "emancipatory knowledge"
    D.   Marx was wrong in maintaining that ideology produces reification

20. Which term is *not* generally associated with Michel Foucault?
    A.   Epistemes
    B.   Archaeology
    C.   Genealogy
    D.* Deconstruction

21. Who is most likely to have written this? "The absence of the transcendental signified extends the domain and the play of signification infinitely."
    A.* Jacques Derrida
    B. Michel Foucault
    C. Jürgen Habermas
    D. Ferdinand de Saussure

22. Who is most likely to have written this? "Civilization, in a general way, constitutes a milieu favorable to the development of madness. If the progress of knowledge dissipates error, it also has the effect of propagating a taste and even a mania for study; the life of the library, abstract speculations, the perpetual agitation of the mind without the exercise of the body, can have the most disastrous effects."
    A.* Michel Foucault
    B. Jacques Derrida
    C. Ferdinand de Saussure
    D. Richard Rorty

23. According to Stephanie Ross, words
    A. Play no role in the way we think about things
    B. Can be painful but are ultimately meaningless
    C.* Structure the way we interact with the world
    D. Hold little interest for feminists

24. Objectification of persons is a moral problem because
    A. More objectification would be a good thing for society
    B. Objects are less attractive than persons
    C. Some people *like* to be objectified
    D.* Objects are the opposite of persons

CHAPTER 14

Eastern Influences

True/False

1. The *Vedas* are the most ancient religious texts of Hinduism.
   T

2. Hindu philosophy, as it has been interpreted over the centuries, is always purely monistic.
   F

3. *Atman* can be defined as "the inner self."
   T

4. *Vishnu* is a personal god worshipped by some Hindus.
   T

5. Buddhism was originally a philosophical response to the question of how the "many" could be "One."
   F

6. The one who attains *nirvana* understands that what is ordinarily thought of as one's body and one's consciousness are not real, not the true Self.
   T

7. *Zen* comes from a Sanskrit word meaning "doctrine."
   F

8. Hui Neng blended Taoist, Confucian, and Buddhist precepts in his philosophy.
   T

9. In Shinto, an ancient native religion of Japan, *kami* referred to the military rulers.
   F

10. In Buddhism, women generally were considered to be of lesser moral worth than men.
    T

11. Murasaki Shikibu rejected mainstream Buddhism's view of women in holding that women should challenge their *karma* and take control of their own lives.
    T

12. Dogen was a Zen monk.
    T

13. Dogen endeavored to set forth a way to achieve permanent joy in *this* life.
    T

14. *Mushin* means the state of "no mind."
    T

15. The art of the samurai warrior is called *haiku*.
    F

16. The perfect samurai closely resembles the Confucian idea of the complete man.
    T

17. Confucius believed that the human person is perfectible.
    T

18. Confucius clearly presented "The Way" as a fixed and eternal principle that transcends and determines the path taken by natural events.
    F

19. The principle of the Mean, for Confucius, meant that one should avoid extremes and seek moderation.
    T

20. Though influential in China, Confucianism never became a state religion.
    F

21. Confucius believed nature is built on a principle of strife that is reflected in human affairs.
    F

22. Before one can help others, said Confucius, he must first cultivate his character by following the examples of superior men from the past.
    T

23. For Confucius, the virtuous character of the sage is molded by habit.
    T

24. Confucius believed a ruler is invariably a model for the behavior of his subjects.
T

25. In Confucian thought, the family must be what today would be called democratic and egalitarian.
F

26. The philosophy of Confucius pictured another world of harmony and joy to which the sage was destined.
F

27. Mencius was a Confucian philosopher.
T

28. Mencius believed human beings are basically good.
T

29. For Mencius, benevolence is at war with its opposite and must be strengthened for the battle.
F

30. Suffering, according to Mencius, is an opportunity for a person to develop a quiet spirit.
T

31. Mencius and Thomas Hobbes, though from widely varying traditions, would agree on their understanding of human nature.
F

32. Though from widely varying traditions, Lao Tzu, the Taoist, and Socrates, the Greek philosopher, had the same estimation of human wisdom.
T

33. Lao Tzu, as did Confucius, sought to directly change society for the better.
F

34. Chuang Tzu believed the sage must dwell in nonaction.
T

35. Within the Tao, said Chuang Tzu, life and death are equal as a single entity.
T

36. Avicenna envisioned God as a Necessary Being.
T

37. Sufism represents the rationalistic strain of Muslim belief.
F

Multiple Choice

38. Which of the following could not be one of the four great sayings of the *Upanishads*?
    A.   Consciousness is *brahman*
    B.* You are you and I am I
    C.   I am *brahman*
    D.   The self is the One

39. An *avatar* is a (an)
    A.* Incarnation
    B.   Religious pendant
    C.   Incense
    D.   Kind of soup

40. Which is *not* one of Buddha's Four Noble Truths?
    A.   There is suffering
    B.* Suffering has no cause
    C.   Suffering can be ended
    D.   Enlightened living can end suffering

41. Which of the following did Buddha believe?
    A.   There is a divine creator
    B.   Salvation must come from God
    C.   Humans must develop the capacity to "cling to" existence
    D.* Humans themselves must cope with the problem of suffering

42. What, for Hui Neng, is *not* a characteristic of the Real Nature?
    A.   It is the eternal and unchanging Tao
    B.* It is pure goodness
    C.   It is an absolute state of "suchness"
    D.   It is neither born nor does it die

43. Which of the following is *not* a teaching of Dogen?
    A.* Permanent joy can only be achieved in the life to come
    B.   Every person has the nature of Buddha
    C.   One must care for others as a parent would
    D.   One must practice the Great Way

44. The word for Zen meditation is
    A.   *Koan*
    B.* *Zazen*
    C.   *Tao*
    D.   None of the above

45. *Yin* is the contractive force. The expansive force is called
    A.   *Chi*
    B.   *Jen*
    C.   *Tao*
    D.*   *Yang*

46. What is *not* true of Murasaki Shikibu?
    A.   She was a feminist philosopher
    B.   She was an adherent of Shinto animism
    C.*   She was a Hindu
    D.   She wrote *Tale of Genji*

47. According to Tsunetomo's *Hagakure*, what makes life so difficult and painful?
    A.   Its brevity
    B.   Its boredom
    C.*   Its uncertainty
    D.   Its seriousness

48. What must the samurai *not* learn?
    A.   To "win beforehand"
    B.   The arts of war
    C.   The arts of peace
    D.*   To know how to rely on others

49. According to the samurai tradition, which of the following is *not* part of the "complete man"?
    A.   He is to avoid luxury
    B.   He should be polite
    C.   He must not lie
    D.*   He must devote himself entirely to practical affairs

50. "Do not do to others what you would not want them to do to you" is a precept of
    A.*   Confucius
    B.   Lao Tzu
    C.   The Buddha
    D.   Dogen

51. Which of the following is *not* a precept of Mencius?
    A.   Only the benevolent ought to be in high stations
    B.   In a state, the people are the most important
    C.   Killing a bad monarch is not murder
    D.*   Virtue alone is sufficient for the exercise of government

52. For Lao Tzu, the Tao is
    A.*   Natural
    B.   Something that can be improved on
    C.   Something only the wise can describe
    D.   Passing away

53. Which would *not* describe the sage, according to Lao Tzu?
    A.   Cautious
    B.   Takes no credit for what is achieved
    C.*   Active
    D.   Has no selfish desire

54. The text describes the sage, as Chuang Tzu saw him, as a
    A.   Bowl
    B.*   Mirror
    C.   Tiger
    D.   Leaf

CHAPTER 15

Other Voices

True/False

1. Much of post-colonial thought takes up the problems of cultural dissolution in the wake of slavery, repression, or marginalization.
   T

2. Post-colonial thought is unified because it is a product exclusively of the Southern Hemisphere.
   F

3. The post-colonial style of analysis is closely tied to concrete historical conditions.
   T

4. In the twentieth century, some kind of Marxism has been the overwhelming theoretical choice among Third World writers.
   T

5. According to the text, there is no such thing as "oral philosophy."
   F

6. The Latin American and British patterns of colonialism were basically the same.
   F

7. The encounter of native peoples with Christianity can be characterized as purely negative.
   F

8. *Ethnophilosophy* is a method of describing the traditional beliefs of a culture.
   T

9. Paulin Hountondji claims that ethnophilosophy and the concept of negritude work against African interests.
   T

10. Léopold Sédar Senghor disputed the claim that there was an "African way of knowing" different from a "European way of knowing."
    F

11. Archbishop Desmond Tutu's method of fighting for the liberation of South Africa from apartheid was through nonviolent action.
    T

12. The Black Power movement in the 1960s continued the assimilationist approach of Booker T. Washington.
    F

13. According to bell hooks, the feminism of the founders of the movement centered on careerism and tended to perpetuate a culture of competition.
    T

14. Chaikh Anta Diop claimed that black Africa was the origin of Egyptian civilization.
    T

15. Molefi Kete Asante is one of the chief architects of Afrocentrism.
    F

16. Carlos Astrada was an Argentinian philosopher.
    T

17. The concept of *Satyagraha* is closely identified with the social and political thinking of Mohandas (Mahatma) Gandhi.
    T

18. Rabindranath Tagore claimed that the traditions of India provide a guide to the complexities of human nature and the behaviors needed for a harmonious and enlightening life.
    T

Multiple Choice

19. Which of the following is *not* a post-colonial thinker?
    A.   Martin Luther King, Jr.
    B.   Fidel Castro
    C.*   Richard Rorty
    D.   Desmond Tutu

20. What is Pan-African philosophy?
    A. The philosophical tradition of Kenya
    B.* A cultural categorization of philosophical activity that includes the work of African thinkers and thinkers of African descent wherever they are located
    C. A cultural categorization of philosophical activity that includes only the work of African thinkers and thinkers of African descent produced within the continent of Africa
    D. All pantheistic African philosophical traditions

21. Who is most likely to have written this? "To my children . . . for whom I dream that one day soon they will no longer be judged by the color of their skin but by the content of their character."
    A. Léopold Sédar Senghor
    B. Desmond Tutu
    C.* Martin Luther King, Jr.
    D. Stokely Carmichael

22. Ontology is that branch of philosophy that concerns itself with
    A.* The question of being
    B. The question of "how should I live in the world?"
    C. The question of "what is truly beautiful?"
    D. The question of "what's for dinner?"

23. Recent feminist thought has been "expanded" to include which of the following concerns of post-colonial writers?
    A. More attention to issues of class
    B. Abandonment of a black-white racial dichotomy
    C. More emphasis on careerism
    D.* Both A and B

24. *Satyagraha* means
    A. "Living comfortably"
    B.* "Clinging to truth"
    C. "Violent overthrow"
    D. "Passive resistance"

25. Which of the following is *not* true of Rabindranath Tagore?
    A. He was a published poet
    B. He was born to an upper-class family in Calcutta, India
    C. He won the Nobel Prize for literature
    D.* He wrote under the pen name of "Mohandas Gandhi"